DESIGN FOR DISCIPLESHIP

D0881658

**Books by J. Dwight Pentecost
available from Kregel Publications**

Design for Discipleship
Things Which Become Sound Doctrine
Thy Kingdom Come

DESIGN FOR DISCIPLESHIP

Discovering God's Blueprint for the Christian Life

J. Dwight Pentecost

kregel
PUBLICATIONS

Grand Rapids, MI 49501

Design for Discipleship: Discovering God's Blueprint for the Christian Life

Copyright © 1996 by J. Dwight Pentecost

Published by Kregel Publications, a division of Kregel, Inc., P.O. Box 2607, Grand Rapids, MI 49501.

Library of Congress Cataloging-in-Publication Data
Pentecost, J. Dwight
  Design for discipleship / by J. Dwight Pentecost.
    p.   cm.
  Originally published: Grand Rapids, Mich.: Zondervan Publishing House, 1971.
    1. Christian life. 2. Sermons, American. I. Title.
BV4501.2.P385   1996   248.4—dc20   95-33414

ISBN 978-0-8254-3451-8

09 10 11 12 13 / 9 8 7 6 5

Printed in the United States of America

To
MOTHER
With Gratitude and Love

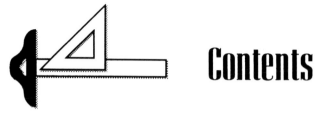

Contents

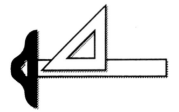

Foreword

The subject of Discipleship is frequently discussed today. Men are called to become disciples without any definition of the concept, and without any clarification of the requirements the Lord makes of those who are His disciples. Hence no intelligent decision can be made concerning this important question. Discipleship is frequently equated with salvation and often erroneously made a condition for becoming a Christian. Thus many are confused about their relationship to Jesus Christ.

In this series of studies the author has attempted to build a Biblical doctrine of discipleship, showing that to become a disciple one must receive a knowledge of divine truth, believe the person presenting the truth, and then completely commit himself to the One presented. He then seeks to show the requirements the Lord Jesus Christ lays upon those who become His disciples so that they may live as His disciples.

Since Jesus Christ came to present God's truth to men, to offer Himself to them as Savior and Lord, and to call them to complete commitment to Him, the subject of discipleship is vitally important if we would understand His person, His call, and His challenge. These messages were first prepared to present to the congregation of Grace Bible Church, of which the author is pastor, to make disciples out of believers. They are presented in this form to bring a wider circle of believers into contact with these important truths.

Deep and abiding appreciation is expressed to Miss Nancy Miller, in whom the pattern of discipleship is displayed, for her labor in preparing the manuscript for publication.

May the Lord be pleased to use this study to bring many who know Him as Savior into an experimental knowledge of Him as Lord.

J. Dwight Pentecost

3909 Swiss Ave.
Dallas, Texas

1 Making Disciples

Matthew 4:18–25

The ministry of Jesus Christ began with the call of Peter and Andrew, and James and John to be disciples; and it closed with the commission given to those whom He called His disciples to go into all the world to make disciples of all nations.

Throughout His ministry Jesus Christ was occupied with making disciples. His ministry was devoted to teaching and training men that these men might be His disciples. From among those who called themselves disciples of the Pharisees and from among others who called themselves disciples of John, and from those who called themselves disciples of Moses, our Lord called men to be disciples of Jesus Christ. His earthly life was invested in these men that they might be His disciples and that they might do the work of a disciple.

Jesus Christ is calling men today to be His disciples. If I asked you if you were a disciple of Jesus Christ, I imagine that almost without exception your answer would be, I am. But before you give an answer I would like you to understand the requirements that Christ lays upon those who would be His disciples. To that end we will devote a number of studies to the subject of the disciples of Jesus Christ, for in the light of New Testament teaching few have any right to claim to be disciples of Jesus Christ; and that profession which we would so glibly make, in light of the demands laid down in the Word of God, would soon prove to be false profession.

There is a vast difference between being saved and being a disciple. Not all men who are saved are disciples although all who are disciples are saved. In discussing the question of discipleship, we are not dealing with a man's salvation. We are dealing with a man's relationship to Jesus Christ as his Teacher, his Master, and his Lord. More than 250 references are made to disciples in the gospels. One cannot read through the gospels that record the earthly life of Jesus Christ without recognizing that the relationship which existed between Christ and these men whom He called to be His disciples was a unique and special relationship. It was a personal and intimate relationship — a relationship based on the knowledge of the person of Christ, a love for the person of Christ, submission to the person of Jesus Christ, and obedience to the commands of Jesus Christ.

The term *disciple* is used in several different ways. Until we are able to distinguish these, we will not comprehend what is involved in discipleship. First of all, the word *disciple* means *a learner, a pupil, a scholar, one who comes to be taught*. The idea of teaching and learning is preeminent in the word *disciple*. In the fourth chapter of the gospel of Matthew as our Lord was walking by the sea, He saw two brothers, Peter and Andrew. They were partners in a fishing business. Later, He saw James, the son of Zebedee, and John, his brother, who were active partners in a lucrative fishing business along with their father. Our Lord summoned these men to Himself, away from the successful pursuits in which they were engaged. He called them to follow Him. They abandoned their nets, forsook their business, and became close followers of Jesus Christ.

Then in Matthew 5:1, we read: "Seeing the multitudes, he went up into a mountain: and when he was set, his disciples came unto him: And he opened his mouth, and taught them." The relationship between Jesus Christ and those who at this point called themselves His disciples was the relationship of teacher to pupil. They were learners. Recognizing themselves to be ignorant and considering Christ the fount of wisdom and knowledge, they turned to Him for instruction. They were what could be called the *curious*. That which characterized them at this point and stage in their development was a curiosity about His words, His doctrine, His teaching. As disciples, pupils who had heard a teacher who differed from any other teacher to whom they had submitted their minds, they were curious about His teaching and about Him as a teacher. They were willing to be taught.

We find in the gospels that the ministry of Christ was largely devoted to teaching, and that teaching was given to multitudes who called themselves His disciples. They testified of Him that never had man spake as this man spake. There were many teachers and rabbis, but this man came with a unique message and a unique method, and they were captivated by His teaching. They were willing to listen to what He had to say. So Christ's ministry was largely a ministry of teaching those who had come to Him as His disciples.

This teaching ministry was undergirded by the ministry of performing miracles. In the fourth chapter of Matthew's gospel, after our Lord had called Peter and Andrew, and James and John, and they had left their ship, their nets, and their father, Jesus Christ (verse 23) "went about all Galilee, teaching in their synagogues, and preaching the gospel of the kingdom, and healing all manner of sickness and all manner of disease among the people." The miracles that Christ performed in His early ministry were to undergird His teaching. His miracles authenticated His message. He had called these men to be His students, and to prove to them that He had the right to teach, He performed miracles. It was only after He had established His authority by the miracles that He performed, that we read in Matthew 5:1, ". . . his disciples came unto him: And he opened his mouth, and taught them." The miracles, then, were subservient to the teaching; the works were subservient to the words.

Great multitudes were willing to attend His teaching; great multitudes were willing to listen to what He taught. Although they were evaluating His words, they made no decision about it. They did not register any acceptance of it; they made no commitment to it; they did not turn from the false teaching of the false teachers in which they had been brought up. But they were willing to continue to listen to Him teach.

We find in Mark 4:34 a reference to this fact: "Without a parable spake he not unto them: and when they were alone, he expounded all things to his disciples." *He expounded all things.* The background of this summary statement is found in the thirteenth chapter of the gospel of Matthew where our Lord gave eight parables to His disciples. We read in Matthew 13:2 that "great multitudes were gathered unto him." Christ taught these multitudes but He taught in the form of parables. "Then," we read in verse 36, "Jesus sent the multitude away, and went into the house: and his disciples came unto him, saying, Declare unto us the parable of the tares of the field. He answered and said unto them. . . ." Christ's exposition of His parables was to those who called themselves His disciples.

We find, again, a reference to this fact in Mark 9:30-32: "They departed thence, and passed through Galilee; and he would not that any man should know it. For he taught his disciples, and said unto them, The Son of man is delivered into the hands of men, and they shall kill him; and after that he is killed, he shall rise the third day. But they understood not that saying, and were afraid to ask him." We find from this line of truth that there were many whom we would call curious ones who were termed disciples, who recognized something new and fresh and unique in Christ's teaching, and who were willing to be taught. Their exercise was an intellectual exercise. They came to be challenged and stimulated intellectually without making any personal commitment to the truth that He was teaching or to the person of the teacher.

We would deduce from a passage such as the sixth chapter of John's gospel where more than 5,000 men, not counting women and children, came together to hear Him teach and to spend all day long sitting at His feet, that the number of the curious who called themselves disciples must have been very large. If Christ could attract a group that numbered more than 5,000, who were willing to spend the entire day to hear Him teach, the multitude of the curious must have been innumerable. That was why the Roman authorities as well as the Jewish authorities were so concerned as to where this movement that Christ was beginning would end; for they could see Christ spreading His doctrine among multitudes that would overthrow the Pharisees and overthrow Rome, and enthrone Jesus Christ. Multitudes who were only curious were called disciples.

Giving ear to the teaching of Christ did not make one a true disciple. We read in John 8:31: "Then said Jesus to those Jews which believed on him, If ye continue in my word, then are ye my disciples indeed." Christ is saying to the curious that simple submission to His voice did not make them disciples — that there must be a reception of the truth, and there must be a response to the truth before they were eligible to be called true disciples.

Today there are multitudes of men who are willing to give their minds to the Word of God to study it as an intellectual pursuit, to listen to what Jesus Christ has to say. And they may even submit themselves to the teaching and preaching of the Scriptures from an evangelical pulpit. But these people have made no response to that truth or to the person of Jesus Christ. They would call themselves disciples of Christ, but Christ disowns them. It is possible to approach the Word simply to have one's intellect stirred, to do what the Athenians did — to listen to some new thing — without any relationship to the truth or without any impact of that truth on one's life. Such a person may call himself a disciple, but on the authority of the Word of God, he is not. He is among the curious who sit to be titillated and tantalized without any response to the truth that is presented. "If ye continue in my word, then are ye my disciples indeed."

But there is a progression from the curious to the *convinced*. These are those who gave themselves perhaps out of curiosity to the Word of God, who had an intellectual curiosity as to what Christ would say and teach, and as they listened to His words and beheld His works, they were convinced of the truth of His word and the truth of His person. They were convinced disciples. I find a reference to this in John 2 at the conclusion of the miracle of the turning of water into wine in Cana of Galilee. John 2:11 records: "This beginning of miracles did Jesus in Cana of Galilee, and manifested forth his glory; and his disciples believed on him." His disciples *believed* on Him. Here were people who had been challenged to follow Him, to listen to Him teach. They had received His teaching; and, when they beheld this miracle, they were convinced of the authority of the person and the truth of His word. John tells us that they believed on Him.

A reference to this is also seen in Matthew 16:13: ". . . he asked his disciples saying, Whom do men say that I the Son of man am?" What explanations have you heard about My words, about My works, about My person? Some identified Him with John the Baptist, some with Elijah, others with Jeremiah or one of the prophets. "He saith unto them, But whom say ye that I am?" The answers being given were answers by the curious. But Christ wanted to see if they had progressed beyond curiosity in their understanding of His person and His words. So He asked them directly, "Whom say ye that I am?" And Simon Peter answered and said, "Thou art the Christ, the Son of the living God." Here is an affirmation of faith in the *person* of Christ. He is the Son of the Living God. It is also an affirmation of faith in the *work* of Christ. He had come to be the Messiah. It was then that Christ pronounced a blessing upon Peter. Why? Because Peter had passed beyond the curious stage to the convinced stage, and he gives this great affirmation that brought our Lord's commendation. He is now a *committed* disciple.

The same truth is emphasized in John 6:67, 68. Multitudes are turning away from Christ because of His inflexible word that men must believe on Him. In verse 67 Jesus said to the twelve, "Will ye also go away? Then Simon Peter answered him, Lord, to whom shall we go? Thou hast the words of eternal life. And we believe and are sure that thou art that Christ, the Son of the living God." What Peter is affirming in this passage is that, in spite of the defection by the curious, there are those who are convinced. They are called disciples because they are convinced of the truth of His person and His work.

Although we have seen that those who are convinced represent a progression beyond the merely curious, we do not yet have our Lord's concept of what constitutes a disciple. For in the gospels discipleship is not the result of the satisfaction of curiosity, nor is it even the result of a conviction that Jesus Christ is truth, and His word is true, although those are prerequisites. One becomes a disciple in the Biblical sense only when one is totally and completely committed to the person of Jesus Christ and His word. Apart from that commitment to Him and His word, one has no right to call himself a disciple of Jesus Christ.

In Luke 9:18 as Christ was praying, His disciples were with Him. To those who called themselves disciples, our Lord laid down the most rigid requirement (verse 23): "He said to them all, If any man will come after me [that is, if any man will be my true disciple], let him deny himself [say no to himself], and take up his cross daily, and follow me. For whosoever will save his life shall lose it: but whosoever will lose his life for my sake, the same shall save it." The key to true discipleship is found in verse 23. Christ said, "If anyone who began as a curious inquirer and consequently called himself a disciple, as a result of exposure to my teaching is convinced that I am the Messiah, the Son of God, and will commit himself totally and completely to Me, that one then becomes My disciple but not until then. If any man will be My disciple, let him say no to himself and take up his cross daily and follow Me."

See it again in Luke 14:27: "Whosoever doth not bear his cross, and come after me, cannot be my disciple." Our Lord had talked a great deal about the cross which He presently would bear when He went to Jerusalem. He laid it down as a stringent requirement: if men were not willing to identify themselves with Him in His rejection and in His death, no matter how convinced they might be of His person or His work, apart from that commitment to Him and identification with Him, they could not be His disciples. He had called them disciples before, and now He says they cannot be His disciples — why the change? Before this they were curious, perhaps even convinced, but not committed; and discipleship depended upon that total, complete commitment to Jesus Christ. Verse 33 of the same chapter says:

"Whosoever he be of you that forsaketh not all that he hath, he cannot be my disciple."

Discipleship involves commitment. It involves identification with Christ in His shameful death. Discipleship involves renunciation of oneself, it involves setting aside one's own aims, goals, ambitions, desires in life. It involves sacrifice for the sake of the Lord Jesus Christ. It involves setting aside one's own will and one's own rights to his life and acknowledging that Jesus Christ has the right to be obeyed, the right to rule. Our Lord said that if a man is not willing to forsake all that he has, he cannot be His disciple.

See how this worked out in John 6: Our Lord had concluded His teaching following the miracle of the feeding of the 5,000; He had fed them with bread from heaven, physical bread, and He reminded them that He had come to provide them with spiritual bread from heaven. He told them that He was the bread of life (verse 48) and that He had come down from heaven to give life (verse 51). He told them (verse 53) that, except they eat His flesh and drink His blood, they would have no life in them. Our Lord pressed them for a decision. They who had been curious now have been convinced, and they must come to the place of a committal. But we read in verses 60-66: "Many therefore of his disciples, when they heard this, said, This is a hard saying; who can hear it? When Jesus knew in himself that his disciples murmured at it, he said unto them, Doth this offend you? What and if ye shall see the Son of man ascend up where he was before? It is the spirit that quickeneth; the flesh profiteth nothing: the words that I speak unto you, they are spirit, and they are life. But there are some of you that believe not. For Jesus knew from the beginning who they were that believed not, and who should betray him. And he said, Therefore said I unto you, that no man can come unto me, except it were given unto him of my Father. [Now notice these words] From that time many of his disciples went back, and walked no more with him."

Who were these defectors? Certainly many were from among the curious who came to hear Him teach, who found that what He taught was too costly and they forsook Him. There were also in that number some who, though they had begun as curious, were convinced that Jesus Christ was the Son of God who had come to reveal truth, to redeem and to reign, but, when it came to giving themselves totally and completely to Him, they abandoned Him and walked with Him no more. These, although they were termed disciples, were not disciples in that New Testament sense that our Lord demanded in Luke 9 and Luke 14, that a disciple is one who has a consuming passion for the person of Christ, whose heart is set upon the person of Christ, who has an unshakeable confidence in the word of Christ and is completely committed to Christ in service and obedience. Intellectual assent to His truth, to His doctrine did not make one a full New Testament disciple. Not until one was willing to commit himself, his life, his mind, his heart, his will to that truth and to the person of Jesus Christ could he be called a disciple of Jesus Christ.

In all honesty before God, would we have to confess that we have stopped somewhere short of that which is the New Testament standard? Discipleship to Jesus Christ means that Jesus Christ has an absolute right to one's life, to do with it as He sees fit; and, while we have given Him certain rights and allowed Him to control in certain phases, we have retained rights to certain areas ourselves. We are not disciples. Discipleship means that Jesus Christ possesses every material thing that I have, it is His. It isn't a question of what I am willing to give to Him; it is a question of what I hold back from Him that is rightfully His; and until I can recognize that everything I have belongs to Jesus Christ, I am not a disciple of Jesus Christ. Jesus Christ has the right to be the one object of my affection; and until Jesus Christ is paramount and pre-eminent in my affections, I am not a disciple of Jesus Christ. Jesus Christ has the right to fill my mind with the knowledge and the truth of Himself, and as long as I let my intellect rule and trust it, I am not a disciple of Jesus Christ.

As long as Christ can reveal His will to me and I choose to debate and to decide whether or not I will do it, I am not a disciple of Jesus Christ. I may have passed from the curious to the convinced, but I am not committed to Him. We repeat it again: a true disciple is one who has a love for the person of Christ, confidence in the word of Christ, and is completely committed to Christ in service and obedience.

According to John 9:28, the blind man whom Christ had healed was reviled by his fellow Jews. They said, "Thou art his disciple; but we are Moses' disciples." Discipleship to Christ is contrasted with discipleship to Moses. How did the nation of Israel become a disciple of Moses? If you think back to the experience of the forefathers in the wilderness, you will recall that God sent Moses to Israel and Moses came with a message from God. Moses authenticated that message by the miracles that substantiated the revelation God had given him. The nation believed Moses because of his word and because of his works. The nation submitted to Moses, and when Moses led them out of Egypt into the wilderness, they followed him. They obeyed Moses.

When Moses told them to go, they went; and when Moses told them to stay, they stayed; when Moses told them to give, they gave. Moses was recognized as God's spokesman. The children of Israel became Moses' disciples because they heard a word, they believed it, they responded to it, and submitted to the authority of Moses.

How had this blind man become a disciple of Jesus? He heard Christ's word, and he saw the sign — he experienced in his own body the miracle of healing. Then he came and threw himself at the feet of Jesus in submission and obedience and worship. He became His disciple by that act of submission.

We do not become disciples simply by satisfying the intellectual curiosity of the curious. We do not become disciples simply because we are convinced of the truth concerning the person and the work of Jesus Christ. We become disciples when we, convinced by the Word of God, commit ourselves totally and completely to Jesus Christ to become His disciples.

Our desire in these studies of the New Testament teaching on discipleship is to unsettle you who have become so comfortable, to disquiet you who have become so satisfied, in order that we might become a people who because of our love for Jesus Christ and submission to His Word, and commitment to His person, are disciples in truth.

2 Call to Discipleship

Matthew 11:25–30

Art thou weary, are thou languid,
Art thou sore distrest?
"Come to Me," saith One, "and, coming,
Be at rest."

To men who were burdened and distressed under the weight and curse of sin and the law, the Lord Jesus Christ came to give freedom and rest. The first word spoken to those who became disciples were the words, "Follow me." And throughout our Lord's life He traveled the highways and byways of the land of Palestine inviting men to come to Him. In Matthew 11:28-30 our Lord summarizes the invitation to discipleship that characterized His earthly ministry: "Come unto me, all ye that labour and are heavy laden, and I will give you rest. Take my yoke upon you, and learn of me; for I am meek and lowly in heart: and ye shall find rest unto your souls. For my yoke is easy and my burden is light."

To understand our Lord's invitation, we must understand that those to whom our Lord was speaking were crushed beneath the weight of the Mosaic law. Our Lord was addressing men who numbered themselves among the disciples of Moses and who were the disciples of the Pharisees. Neither Moses nor the Pharisees could give rest from the pressing burden or release from the oppressive load that the law and Judaism placed upon men. Recognizing that there was no other course to rest and peace than that to be found through submission to Himself, Christ came to invite men out of their old discipleship to a new discipleship.

The law was given by Moses (John 1:17). Men submitted themselves to the law and, by submitting themselves to the law, became
disciples of the law or disciples of the lawgiver, that is, disciples of
Moses. This fact is attested by John 9:28 where, in response to the
testimony of the man born blind, the leaders in Israel said, "Thou art
his disciple; but we are Moses' disciples." Those who recognized an
obligation to the law and submitted themselves to rule by the law were
called the disciples of the law. They became disciples of the law or
disciples of Moses by submitting to the authority of Moses and the
Mosaic law.

The Pharisees had devised a system in which they had codified the
Mosaic law into some 365 prohibitions and 250 commandments. They
required those who followed them to submit to their interpretations
of this law. Because the Pharisees considered themselves the official
interpreters of the law, they promoted themselves to a position of
authority in Israel. In Matthew 23:2, Christ referred to the Scribes
and the Pharisees as men who "sit in Moses' seat." Claiming the authority of Moses as interpreters and teachers of the law, they demanded
that all in Israel who submitted to Moses also submit themselves to
them. They demanded that men by submission become disciples of
the Pharisees, and that individuals in Israel recognize themselves not
only as disciples of Moses but also as disciples of the Pharisees. This
is seen in a passage such as Mark 2:18 where Christ is asked the
question, "The disciples of John and of the Pharisees used to fast:
and they come and say unto him, Why do the disciples of John and
of the Pharisees fast, but thy disciples fast not?" This shows us that
those who submitted themselves to the Pharisees were disciples of the
Pharisees. They became disciples by voluntarily submitting themselves
to the rule of the Pharisees over them.

When the law was imposed on a man, it did not bring liberty. It
brought bondage. Rather than freedom, it brought oppression. Instead of a sense of release, it brought a sense of guilt and failure.
The leaders of the Pharisees made no effort to bring freedom and
liberty and release to those who were their disciples. The system of
the Pharisees, according to Matthew 23:4, imposed heavy burdens
that were grievous to be borne; for our Lord, characterizing the Pharisees, said, "They bind heavy burdens and grievous to be borne, and
lay them on men's shoulders; but they themselves will not move them
with one of their fingers." Our Lord looked at a nation of men who
had become disciples of Moses and disciples of the Pharisees by a
voluntary submission to their authority. He saw that nation as under

a heavy burden, a burden that was grievous to be borne, a burden that the Pharisees made no effort to lift from those who were crushed beneath its load. Our Lord came to say, "Come unto me . . . and I will give you rest."

Those who were under the Mosaic law were said to be yoked to Moses. Those who were under the authority of the Pharisees were said to be yoked to the Pharisees. This is evidenced when we turn to Acts 15 where we have recorded the word of Peter after the Day of Pentecost as he discusses the question as to whether Gentiles who were being saved should be compelled to be circumcised. That was another way of asking whether believers in the new era would have to submit to the authority of the law or would have to be yoked with Moses. In verse 7 we read, "Men and brethren, ye know how that a good while ago God made choice among us, that the Gentiles by my mouth should hear the word of the gospel, and believe. And God, which knoweth the hearts, bare them witness, giving them the Holy Ghost, even as he did unto us; And put no difference between us and them, purifying their hearts by faith. Now therefore why tempt ye God, to put a yoke upon the neck of the disciples, which neither our fathers nor we were able to bear?" Notice the words in verse 10. When they considered imposing the law, the Mosaic system, on believers in Jesus Christ, men who had been saved by faith, Peter said that would be imposing a yoke on them that neither they nor their fathers were able to bear.

When Christ in Matthew 11:29 is talking about a yoke from which He will deliver men, He is talking about the yoke of the law, the yoke of Pharisaism that put a heavy burden, too grievous to be borne, upon the necks of men. Christ, coming to those who were so crushed, offers them release, liberty, freedom, rest. Notice our Lord's invitation, in Matthew 11:28 when He says to this oppressed multitude, "Come unto me." Moses offered the children of Israel the law at Mount Sinai. According to Exodus 19:8 Israel said, "All that the Lord hath spoken we will do." They voluntarily submitted themselves to the law and were yoked to the law. The Pharisees imposed authority over the nation of Israel and the nation voluntarily submitted to the authority of the Pharisees. They had done the bidding of the Pharisees when the Pharisees had said, "Come unto me." Now our Lord stands and says to an oppressed, burdened people, "Come unto me."

This is the same invitation our Lord had given to the first apostles. In Mark 1:16, 17 we read that Christ saw "Simon and Andrew his brother casting a net into the sea: for they were fishers. And Jesus said unto them, Come ye after me." And in verse 19, "He saw James the son of Zebedee, and John his brother, who also were in the ship mending their nets. And straightway he called them: and they left their father Zebedee in the ship with the hired servants, and went after him." Peter and Andrew and James and John became disciples by heeding our Lord's invitation when He said, "Follow me. Come unto me."

In John 1:37 Jesus again is inviting men to Himself, "And the two disciples heard him speak, and they followed Jesus." In verse 38 they asked, "Rabbi, where dwellest thou?" He said unto them, "Come and see. They came and saw. . . ." Again in verse 43, Jesus "findeth Philip and saith unto him, Follow me." And Philip followed. Here the number of disciples was expanded from the original four because Christ presented Himself to them and said, "Follow me." And they submitted to Him and followed. Now in Matthew 11:28 and much later in His ministry after He had completed the call of the original twelve, Christ stood and said, "Come unto me." He was not calling them to a system. This was not calling them to a religion. Nor was He calling them to a table of stone or to the traditions of men, asking men to submit to those. He was calling men to a Person, to Himself. Discipleship is the response of an individual to a Person who stands before believers and says, "Come unto me."

You will notice the universality of this invitation, "Come unto me, all ye that labour and are heavy laden." In Israel there could not be found one who had found rest through the Levitical system, who had found rest through Pharisaism, who had found rest through the multiplied works in which he was involved. Through the multitude of sacrifices which he offered on Jewish altars, not one had found rest. All were burdened, all guilty, all condemned. Christ opened the invitation to all the burdened and oppressed, none excluded. "Come unto me, *all* ye that labour and are heavy laden." And the verse concludes with Christ's promise, "I will give you rest."

Rest for the oxen who had been laboring in the yoke all day was found only when the owner took the ox to the stable and removed the yoke so that the ox might feed and drink. As long as the ox was in the yoke, he was under the burden of the yoke. The removal of the yoke meant rest.

There could be no rest to the burdened and the oppressed until Christ lifted the weight of the yoke of the law and the yoke of Pharisaism from them. Christ could give no release to men until He delivered them from the bondage to which they had submitted themselves when they became disciples of Moses and disciples of the Pharisees. "Come unto me, all ye that labour and are heavy laden, and I will give you rest."

How could Christ give rest? The strange contradiction is that Christ exchanges the yoke of Mosaism, the yoke of Pharisaism, for another yoke. "Take my yoke upon you" is the means by which men find rest. The questioner might well ask, "If I must bear a yoke, what difference does it really make whether it be the yoke of Mosaism or Pharisaism or the yoke of Christ? After all, a yoke is a yoke." Christ did not say unto the distressed, "Come unto Me, and I will remove all yokes from you and give you rest." His invitation and the condition upon which man would experience the results were found in taking "my yoke upon you." To take Christ's yoke means to submit yourself to the authority of Christ. It means to put yourself under His rule, to join yourself together with Him. He is inviting men to put their shoulders into a new yoke, a new yoke in which He is the yoke mate. And He promises that, as they submit to His authority and are yoked with Him, they will find rest unto their souls.

The reason men find rest by taking Christ's yoke is that His yoke is a different kind of yoke. The yoke of the Pharisees was an obligation to observe the traditions of men. The yoke of the law was to observe all that the law commanded, and refrain from all it prohibited. But Christ said He was offering them a new kind of yoke and His yoke is easy and His burden is light. As one is bound in this new kind of yoke, Christ could promise that "Ye shall find rest unto your souls." The yoke to which Christ invited men, when borne as a co-laborer with Jesus Christ, is no burden at all. It is a source of rest, satisfaction, enjoyment and contentment. The Christian life, the life of a disciple, is not a life of passivity or inactivity. It is a life of activity because the life of Christ works itself out through the true disciple of Jesus Christ. Christ is our life and He is our strength. As one is yoked to Jesus Christ that which is performed is the joy of the true disciple.

Back in my college days I observed an incident that made this Scripture very clear to me. On Sunday afternoons I used to go out to a little rural Sunday school to teach. One afternoon the superintendent of the Sunday school, a farmer, and I were visiting in the community. There was an old farmer plowing with a team of oxen. As I saw this team I was somewhat amazed, for one was a huge ox and the other a very small bullock. That ox towered over the little bullock that was sharing the work with him. I was amazed and perplexed to see a farmer trying to plow with two such unequal animals in the yoke and commented on the inequality to the man with whom I was riding. He stopped his car and said, "I want you to notice something. See the way those traces are hooked to the yoke? You will observe that the large ox is pulling all the weight. That little bullock is being broken into the yoke but he is not actually pulling any weight." My mind instinctively came to this passage of Scripture where our Lord said, "Take my yoke upon you, and learn of me; for I am meek and lowly in heart: and ye shall find rest unto your souls." In the normal yoke, the load is equally distributed between the two that are yoked together, but when we are yoked with Jesus Christ, He bears the load and we who are yoked with Him share in the joy and the accomplishment of the labor but without the burden of the yoke. The tragedy is that some of us have never been broken in to the yoke.

How could a man submit to Christ's yoke? How can he take Christ's yoke upon him? The explanation is in the little words, "Learn of me." We may paraphrase it: let Me teach you what you need to know. Let Me guide you and direct you in your activities. Let Me set the direction of your life. "Learn of me." The Jews to whom our Lord spoke had been taught by the Pharisees who themselves transmitted the traditions of men, and they were bound by the traditions that they had learned from the Pharisees. They had learned from their masters. These Jews were so burdened by the law that they would not step across a grassy plot on the Sabbath Day. Do you know why? The law said, "Remember the sabbath day, to keep it holy. . . . in it thou shalt not do any work." That meant a man could not sow in his field. They had so interpreted the law that, if a man stepped upon a plot of grass and knocked some ripe seed from the seedpod onto the ground, he was guilty of sowing upon the Sabbath Day. Pharisaism taught that it was wrong for a man who wore false teeth six days a week to wear them on the seventh day, for that was bearing a burden and was a violation of the Sabbath Day. The Pharisees taught that it was wrong to use any internal medication for healing on the Sabbath Day. If a man broke his arm, you could put it into a splint; that was external. Or if he had a severe toothache, you could give him a sip of wine to deaden the pain as long as he spit out the wine and washed his mouth out. If he did not wash his mouth out, he might inadvertently swallow a bit of that wine, which became internal medication and that made him a Sabbath violator.

The disciples of the Pharisees had learned the burden that the law imposed. Now Christ said they were going to have to unlearn all they had learned. Let Me teach you. If you follow the gospel record you will find that from this point on in our Lord's life He concentrates, not on performing miracles, but on teaching men the truth that they needed to know about the Father, about Himself, about the way of life and about the way of salvation. Man must make a choice. Men must make a decision whether they will continue as disciples of the Pharisees or whether they will submit to His Word, submit to His teaching, submit themselves to His authority and become His disciples.

Beloved of God, who have been redeemed by the blood of Christ, this word is directed to you. We affirm again that it is possible for a man to be saved without being a disciple of Jesus Christ. A believer becomes a disciple of Jesus Christ when he submits to the authority of Christ's word and acknowledges Christ's right to rule over him, puts himself totally and completely at the disposal of Jesus Christ. An ox does not accidentally slip into a yoke. He has to submit to it. You will not somehow fall into discipleship. You become a disciple when you before God register a decision of your will in which you declare you are submitting yourself to Jesus Christ, you are putting yourself under the authority and control of His Word, and you accept His Word as the law of your life, and by the Spirit's power live by it.

Many of us have no right to call ourselves disciples. When Christ said, "Come unto me, all ye that labour and are heavy laden, and I will give you rest," we have responded and have come to Him. But when He prepares to slip a yoke around our necks to join us to Himself, we resist, we fight, we back off. We refuse to be brought under bondage to anyone, not even to Jesus Christ. Until you become yoked to Jesus Christ in the sweetest bondage that heaven or earth knows, you cannot be a disciple. "Take my yoke upon you" means learn of Me, submit to My Word, acknowledge the authority of My Person, and when you do that, and only when you do that, "ye shall find rest unto your souls."

Are you restless, child of God? Disturbed? Often distraught, discouraged? Perchance at the edge of despair? Put your shoulder into His yoke in order that He might bear the burden. Learn to walk yoked to Jesus Christ, and you shall find rest for your soul. This is His promise.

3 Becoming a Disciple

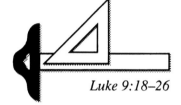

Luke 9:18–26

The Lord Jesus, in calling His first disciples, had called men from comparatively insignificant and obscure backgrounds to Himself. They, by virtue of their association with Him, had been catapulted into a position of prominence. Because of our Lord's words and His works, the entire nation was influenced by the ministry of the Lord Jesus Christ. From border to border the name of Jesus of Nazareth had become a household word as men debated the question of His authority and of His person. Our Lord had set the twelve apart to special ministries. These ministries are outlined in the ninth chapter of the gospel of Luke. There the Lord, after calling together His Twelve, gave them power and authority over all demons and to cure diseases.

They were given power from God to perform miracles to authenticate their message and, in this, they were likened to Moses and Elijah in the Old Testament. For, when God sent a message to Israel through those chosen ones, He gave Moses the power to perform miracles in Egypt and Elijah to perform miracles in the presence of the nation Israel to authenticate their message concerning redemption from God and judgment to come. The Twelve enjoyed a privilege that had previously belonged only to those worthies in the Old Testament.

Our Lord further, according to the second verse, sent these, who had been given this authority out to preach the message of the kingdom of God. As the Twelve went to preach, they were performing a ministry like that of Isaiah or Jeremiah or Ezekiel or Zechariah. They might well have taken pride in the position and the privilege that was given to them as they were joined to that select group, the honored prophets who had preceded them.

In the third and fourth verses we find that our Lord had given to these whom He had called, commissioned, empowered and sent, the right to receive support from those to whom they ministered. They were told that, as they went to preach, they were to "Take nothing for your journey, neither staves, nor scrip, neither bread, neither money; neither have two coats apiece. And whatsoever house ye enter into, there abide, and thence depart." Those who received the message would receive the messengers and contribute to their physical and material needs so that every need might be met. In this privilege conferred upon them they were likened to the priests of the Old Testament because no priest was responsible for his own support. He was to live from the sacrifices that were brought as offerings to God. God had assumed the support of those who served in a priestly ministry, and the nation Israel recognized the right of the priest to be supported by those to whom they ministered. To no other class was this privilege given in the Old Testament, and these chosen ones were set apart to receive support as the priests receive support. In this they were likened to Aaron and Aaron's sons in the Old Testament.

We find further, according to the fifth verse, that to them was given the right to judge and to pronounce a message of judgment from God upon those who rejected their message of the good news that the Redeemer had come. We read in the fifth verse, "Whosoever will not receive you, when ye go out of that city, shake off the very dust from your feet for a testimony against them." The shaking off of the dust of the feet was a sign of condemnation and consignment to judgment. These who had been set apart to judge had the same authority conferred upon them that the kings of the Old Testament had had conferred by God, for the kings were raised up to be administrators of government. To them was committed the responsibility of not only rewarding those who did good but also of punishing those who were evildoers. The sentence of judgment was on their lips by divine authority. And we find that the Twelve were given the same authority that belonged to David or to Solomon or the godly King Josiah, or any others who sat by divine appointment on the throne of David.

These who had received authority to preach, to authenticate their preaching by miracles, to be sustained in the ministry and to pronounce judgment on those who rejected their message, had a fruitful ministry. According to verse six, they went everywhere preaching the Gospel and healing. So widespread was their ministry that the whole land was confronted with the fact that God had sent a Messiah to redeem His people. The news of the message even penetrated the recesses of the governor's palace, where Herod the Tetrarch heard the message of Jesus Christ as witness was borne to him of the ministry of Christ and the message of Christ by the messengers whom Jesus Christ had sent out. When the Twelve returned to our Lord from their ministry throughout the land, according to the tenth verse, they could report a successful ministry: ". . . the apostles, when they were returned, told him all that they had done."

There was one other privilege that was afforded the Twelve. We see that referred to in verses 18 - 21. They received a revelation of divine truth. Christ had been offering Himself as a Redeemer and a King to Israel. Men had been debating the question of the person of Christ and the authority by which He preached. Christ asked the disciples after their return from their itinerating ministry to report on the responses to His own presentation of His person. The disciples came back to report that they had heard some men say that He was John the Baptist; others reported He was Elijah; others reported He was one of the prophets. All of these men mentioned had come from God and operated by divine authority in their ministry. Our Lord turned to the Twelve with the question, "But whom say ye that I am?" And Peter, as the spokesman for the Twelve, gave his great confession of faith in the person and work of Christ as he said, "The Christ of God" or as Matthew records it, "Thou art the Christ, the Son of the living God."

That knowledge did not come by natural perception; it was. a fact revealed to Peter directly from God Himself, for in Matthew 16:17 it is recorded that our Lord said, "Blessed art thou, Simon Bar-jona; for flesh and blood hath not revealed it unto thee, but my Father which is in heaven [hath revealed it unto thee]." The disciples had received special revelation from God concerning the person and work of Christ. In this the disciples were likened to the prophets of the Old Testament to whom the Lord had appeared, to whom He had delivered His word. We think, for instance, of Daniel away from his homeland as a captive in Babylon to whom God appeared and spoke to reveal intimate details concerning the coming of the Redeemer. Think, too, of Isaiah to whom the word of the Lord came describing the character and the work of the Lord Jesus Christ centuries before He appeared. Or of the prophet Zechariah who could say, "The word of the Lord came to me," a word that brought a specific revelation concerning the work which the Lord Jesus would do when He came to redeem men.

It is obvious from the record given to us in the ninth chapter of the book of Luke that these Twelve were given special privileges and responsibilities. Yet in Luke 9:23 our Lord made certain demands of those who had been so privileged, for He said to them *all* (to the very ones who had received this revelation, who had received this authority, who were given the privileges of preaching the Gospel and being supported by it, who could pronounce judgment from God upon the rejectors), "If any man will come after me, let him deny himself, and take up his cross daily, and follow me." Receiving revelation did not make them disciples. Power to perform miracles did not make them disciples. A commission to preach did not make them disciples. Receiving authority to pronounce judgment did not make them disciples. Being given the right to receive support in their ministry did not make them disciples. Our Lord said, "If any man will come after me [that is as My disciple], he must deny himself, and take up his cross daily and follow me." Discipleship did not depend on what they received from Christ; it depended on a committal of themselves to Jesus Christ. To get that lesson across to them, our Lord said, "Let him deny himself, and take up his cross daily, and follow me."

There were two parts to the requirement that our Lord laid upon these men if they were to be true disciples. The first or the negative side is found in the words, "let him deny himself. . . ." The great danger that would confront these men after their highly successful ministry in the name of Christ was that they would be lifted up in pride. The position they held, the truth that they knew, the productivity of their ministry, the privileges to which they were introduced would produce pride in the flesh. It would have been so easy for them to report to the One who had sent them out and to turn around and go out again to try to repeat the same ministry. And it would have been just as easy for them to trust the revelation which had been given as sufficient and final, to traffic in the authority to cast out demons that had been given to them. Thus they could proceed on the basis of a commission to preach without any committal to the person who had revealed Himself and given them His own authority, and then commissioned them to bear His message.

If a man is to be a disciple of Jesus Christ, he must set himself aside totally and completely; to know nothing of himself, to have no will of his own concerning his own life, to have no affection to which he gives his heart. Our Lord's demands were absolute and final.

As long as a man proceeds on the basis of natural reasoning, even though he applies his natural reasoning to the Word of God, he cannot be a disciple because he has not denied the place of his natural mind in the reception of divine truth. As long as a man pursues the affections of his natural heart, he cannot be a disciple of Jesus Christ, for to be a disciple his affections must be set on things above. As long as a man pursues his own will and does that which pleases him, he cannot be a disciple of Jesus Christ because a disciple must submit completely to the Master's will. The Master desires to put His own truth into the mind of the disciple and His own affections into the heart of the disciple. He puts His own will before the disciple so that the disciple knows nothing, loves nothing, obeys no one other than the Lord Jesus Christ. He must deny himself.

The second aspect is the positive aspect. The disciple must take up his cross daily and follow Christ. The cross as an instrument of torture and punishment was a cruel device of the Romans. Unknown among men before, the cross was devised as a means of capital punishment by the Romans, to give vent to their bloodthirstiness and barbarism. Among all peoples, the cross was held to be a despicable form of torture and death. It was held in contempt by all men, and even the bloodthirsty Romans reserved this for only the lowest of criminals. That this is the view the world had of the cross is testified to by the Apostle Paul when, in Galatians 3:13, he says, "Christ hath redeemed us from the curse of the law, being made a curse for us: for it is written, Cursed is every one that hangeth on a tree."

A special curse was pronounced upon a man who died this despicable death. In writing to the Philippians, to present the mind of Christ as a mind that was totally and completely subservient to the will of God, Paul testifies of Jesus Christ (2:8): "Being found in fashion as a man, he humbled himself, and became obedient unto death, even the death of the cross." To the Apostle Paul, that Jesus Christ would give Himself in death to be obedient to God was singular and significant, but that Jesus Christ would be obedient even though it entailed death on the cross, was beyond human imagination. We affirm then that not only the concept of the New Testament but the concept of the world as a whole was that the cross was an emblem of shame.

Now Christ asks a man to identify himself with that which to the world speaks of shame. Jesus Christ in the Old Testament was described as the despised and rejected one. He was despised and rejected because of the circumstances of His birth, for, since natural men could not understand the Virgin Birth, they concluded that His mother was

guilty of immorality. Also, He was despised and rejected because of
the circumstances of His early life. Separated from the privileges that
abounded in Jerusalem, growing up in a military post town, He was
looked down upon by the rest of the citizens of the nation. Jesus was
despised and rejected because, when He came to introduce Himself to
the nation, He was not introduced by a highly respected priest or an
acknowledged prophet but was introduced by one who was himself
an outcast from Israel. John the Baptist, His forerunner, was a renegade
from a priest's family who led a rebellious movement out in the wilderness. Jesus was despised and rejected in His ministry because He
condemned the establishment, saying there was no life in Pharisaism,
calling men to Himself. He was despised and rejected in His death
because He was numbered among the transgressors, because He was
consigned to death on the tree.

Well does Isaiah summarize His life from birth to death, "He is
despised and rejected of men; a man of sorrows, and acquainted with
grief: and we hid as it were our faces from him; he was despised,
and we esteemed him not" (53:3). Jesus Christ, in asking men to take
up His cross, is asking them to identify themselves with Him as the
despised and rejected One. He is asking men to assume for themselves
the burden of being despised and rejected as He is despised and rejected. There could not help but be the guilt by association. Christ
knew that, and the disciples knew that — yet He asked them to identify
themselves with Him and partake of that which was the attitude of
the nation toward Him.

The cross in the life of Jesus Christ was the manifestation of the will
of God for Him. Christ bore the cross not because He had a martyr
complex and welcomed death, not that He might move men to compassion by the extent of His suffering. Jesus Christ bore the cross
because that was God's will for Him. When God asks a man to take
up his cross, God is asking a man for Jesus' sake and in Jesus' name
to accept whatever manifestation of His will God sets before that individual. Your cross and my cross and Christ's cross will all be different.
God's will for Jesus Christ was to go to the cross to die. God had no
such will for any other individual in the history of the human race,
and He never will. His cross for you is not for you to die on Calvary,
but His plan for you is as definite and specific as His will was for
Jesus Christ. Discipleship is dependent upon a willingness to accept
God's will as God makes it known to you and to identify yourself
with Jesus Christ in the discharge of that will. That makes one a
disciple.

In essence, Jesus is saying, "If any man will come after Me as My true disciple, let him say no to himself (for thus the word reads literally), set aside his own will, and take up his cross as I took up My cross in obedience to the will of God, and come and follow Me."

Our Lord is asking for a decision. He was asking for a specific act of dedication, a definite committal when He said, " . . . let him deny himself, and take up his cross." This is the background in the mind of the Apostle Paul as he writes in the twelfth chapter of Romans. After he has outlined all that the Son of God has done in obedience to the will of God to provide both justification and sanctification for men, the apostle comes to this exhortation, "I beseech you therefore, brethren, by [or in view] of the merices of God [that is mercies that have provided salvation, justification, sanctification], that ye present your bodies a living sacrifice." This presentation is the reasonable, logical and spiritual obligation resting on the child of God because of what God has done, and is viewed as a definite, specific act. Present your bodies. Apart from this specific committal, although one is born again because of his faith in Jesus Christ, he is not a disciple of Jesus Christ. He may know a good deal of divine truth because of his study in the Word, he may have been a witness to Jesus Christ as he has propagated the Word, he may exercise some authority in the body of believers, but apart from this specific commitment to Jesus Christ, he is not a disciple.

The word *present* is the word that was used in the marriage ceremony. It referred to that specific act when the father of the bride would take his daughter's hand and put it into the hand of the father of the groom. The father of the groom, in turn, would take that hand and put it into the hand of his son, the bridegroom. That was called *the presentation.* It was at that moment that the bride became the wife.

There comes a moment in the marriage ceremony when I as an officiating pastor ask the young man standing before me, "Wilt thou have this woman to be thy wife?" And he replies, "I will." I turn to the bride and say, "Wilt thou have this man to be thy husband?" And she says, "I will." And I proceed to say, " I pronounce you man and wife." What was it that made them husband and wife? It was not my pronouncement. I could only pronounce in keeping with the facts. They became husband and wife when they presented themselves one to the other by a specific, definite act of the will.

I might ask an unmarried person, "Do you want to be married?" I would get an affirmative reply. But that desire to be married does not make one married. I might ask one who answered in the affirmative, "Do you have the young man or the young woman already selected, and have you an understanding with him or her?" And that person might say, "Yes." But his understanding and expectation of a future relationship does not make him married. One is not married apart from a consent of the will to be married, apart from a presentation of one to the other.

I might ask, "Do you want to be a disciple of Jesus Christ?" You would say, "Yes, I want to be a disciple of Jesus Christ." But until you present yourself in a definite act to Jesus Christ, you are not a disciple. Born again through faith in Jesus Christ, yes; saved, yes; saved forever, yes; a disciple, no. It is not the question of how much you know or how much you do, or what authority you have. It is the question of presentation that determines discipleship.

During the course of our studies of this question of discipleship, a reader may have said in his heart, "I want to be a disciple." He may even have prayed, "Lord, make me a disciple." But his desire, his praying would not make him a disciple. Only the offering of himself to Jesus Christ, only the committal of himself to Jesus Christ to be a disciple of His, makes one a disciple.

Some of you readers have been in a state of indecision long enough, and it is time you came to that place of definite committal to Jesus Christ, making you a true disciple. You know something of what is entailed. A disciple, first of all, must be redeemed by the blood of Christ. He is one who is taught the Word of Christ and obeys the Word; he submits to the authority of Christ. A disciple is one who serves Christ. He is one who is separated from the world that hates Christ. A disciple is one who is characterized by the love of Christ. Now the question directly addressed to you is this: "Are you willing to give yourself to Jesus Christ to be His disciple?"

This is Christ's invitation, "If any man will come after me, let him deny himself, take up his cross daily, and follow me." "Come unto me all ye that labour and are heavy laden, and I will give you rest. Take my yoke upon you, and learn of me; for I am meek and lowly in heart: and ye shall find rest unto your souls." What is your response?

4 Obedience and Discipleship

Luke 9:57–62

It does not take much of a man to be a disciple, but it takes all of him that there is. Our Lord said, "Not every one that saith unto me, Lord, Lord, shall enter into the kingdom of heaven, but he that doeth the will of my Father" (Matthew 7:21). One requirement which Jesus Christ laid down for disciples was that of obedience — absolute, unquestioned, implicit obedience. Apart from obedience, one has no right to call himself a disciple of Jesus Christ.

To illustrate this, our Lord told a parable which is recorded in the twenty-first chapter of Matthew beginning at verse 28. A certain man had two sons. He came to the first and said, "Son, go work today in my vineyard." The father gave a command to the son, revealing his will to the son. There was no doubt about the instruction and there was no confusion in the command that was given. The father's will was for the son to go to work in his vineyard. The son recognized a responsibility to this revelation of the will of the father, for he said, "I will not," but afterward he repented and went. Then the father came to the second son with the same command and he answered, "I go, sir," and went not. The one at first disclaimed obedience but then obeyed the will of the father and went and labored. The other promised obedience but was disobedient and did not fulfill the command of the father.

After having told the story, Christ asked the question: "Whether of the twain did the will of his father? They said unto him, the first."

It was not profession that demonstrated relationship to the will of the father, it was the act of obedience. One was an obedient son in spite of his profession; the other was a disobedient son in spite of his profession. It is not the words on one's lips that make him a disciple of Jesus Christ; it is obedience to the revelation of the will of God that makes one a disciple of Jesus Christ. In exploring the New Testament teaching on discipleship, we would like to deal with this subject of discipleship and obedience.

In a previous study we saw that the word *disciple* is used in several different senses in the New Testament. First of all it is used of those who were simply curious about our Lord's teaching. Seeing the miracles that He did as He ministered in Galilee, they knew that behind His miracle was an explanation and interpretation. Curious as to what He would say, they came to listen to Him teach. They were what we would call students, learners, or those who came to be taught.

Then in the second place we found that there were those called disciples who were convinced of the truth of what Christ had to say. They listened to His words and they realized that these expressions were not of human wisdom; and they were convinced that He was from God and spoke the truth of God.

In a third sense, however, the disciples were those who, after they were convinced of the truth of the word, completely committed themselves to the Person who had taught them. If one stops short of this total, complete commitment to the Person of Jesus Christ, he is not a disciple of Jesus Christ. He may be numbered among the curious, or he may even have progressed to the place where he is convinced of the truth of what Christ had to say or of what God's Word says, but until he completely commits himself to the Person whose word he has come to believe, he is not a disciple in the full New Testament sense of the word.

A lady once came to me after I had presented this truth. She said, "After hearing your sermon I don't believe there are many disciples." Then she continued, "I don't know even whether you are a disciple." I trust that the Spirit of God will bring that same searching of heart to each one of us as we examine our relationship to the Person of Jesus Christ in the light of the demands of the Word of God.

How hypocritical it is to profess to be a disciple and be characterized by disobedience. While one is in the place of disobedience, he is not in the place of discipleship, for the Bible demands absolute obedience to the Word of God and the authority of Jesus Christ as a necessary prerequisite to discipleship.

In Luke 9:23 our Lord taught, "If any man will come after me, let him deny himself, and take up his cross daily, and follow me." Let him deny himself. The word translated *deny* is a very strong word in the original text which literally might be translated *say no to oneself*. Within each one of us a contest is going on. It is a contest for mastery, contest for the right to rule. When Jesus Christ redeems a man through His death, that man becomes the purchased possession of Jesus Christ. Since we belong to Jesus Christ by purchase, He has an absolute right to dominate and to control. That is why the Apostle Paul chose to introduce himself as the bondslave of Jesus Christ. He viewed himself as one who had been purchased by another and had become the property of another.

A bondservant rightly has no will of his own. He is not given the prerogative of debating the commands that come from his master; he is not responsible to determine the course of his conduct. That is the right and the responsibility of the one who is his master. But bondslaves are by nature rebels. And we are rebels against the authority of Christ; we delight to superimpose our will against the will of Christ and to sit in judgment upon that which is the revelation of the will of God for us. In so doing, we leave the place of obedience, the place of submission, the place of discipleship. "If any man will come after me [that is, become my disciple in truth and in deed]; let him deny himself [set aside any rights to his own person, to his own mind, to his own will, to his own counsel], and follow me [identify himself with the rejected one, and follow where he leads and directs in perfect obedience]."

When Christ summoned Peter, James, John and Andrew to be disciples, it meant they must forsake their nets and their boats, and the lucrative fishing business in which they were engaged. They forsook their former lives immediately to become disciples. When Christ called Matthew, it meant that he had to forsake the tax-collector's office with the remuneration and the responsibility that went with it. The day Christ called Matthew to become His disciple, Matthew forsook all and followed Him.

When Christ called Philip, the evangelist, according to the Book of Acts he was engaged in a very fruitful ministry in Samaria. It meant that he forsook Samaria and the ministry in which he was engaged to go down into the desert place alone. Philip left Samaria.

When Christ called Paul to be a disciple, it meant he had to give up the privileges and prerogatives of being one of the hierarchy in

Jerusalem. But until he was willing to forsake all he could not be a disciple.

The same ninth chapter of the gospel of Luke that lays down the requirement: let a man deny himself and follow Me in perfect obedience, gives us a number of illustrations of those who refuse to obey. Look at the tests that were put before individuals who were being called to be disciples of Jesus Christ. We see how men offered excuse after excuse and found reason after reason why they should not submit their wills to the will of Christ and walk in perfect obedience before Him.

What is given in verses 51 - 62 was designed to illustrate the principle that Christ laid down in Luke 9:23. Here are individuals who were called to become disciples, who were invited to commit themselves totally to the Person of Jesus Christ, believe His word and obey His will. But for one reason or another they turned from that complete commitment to the Person of Christ, doubted the word of Christ and rejected the will of Christ. While these thoughts are not exhaustive nor will you find an absolute parellel in them to your own experience, yet they will illustrate the ways men find to circumvent that which is necessary in becoming a disciple of Jesus Christ.

Christ was on His way to Jerusalem and He chose to go from Galilee up to Jerusalem through Samaria. Hostility had existed between the Jews and the Samaritans since the time of Ezra and Nehemiah, the time of the restoration of the remnant from the Babylonian captivity. This animosity had arisen at the time the Jews, occupied in the work of rebuilding the temple in Jerusalem, had resisted the proffered help of that half-caste group of Samaritans, a people of mixed origin, a mixture of Jews who had been left in the land and their Assyrian captors. They had set up their own independent religious system, not recognizing the temple in Jerusalem. Having set up their own temple in Mt. Gerizim, they did not recognize the prophets that God had sent to Judah and to Israel; they recognized only Moses and the five books of Moses. They did not recognize the Aaronic priesthood; they had set up their own independent priesthood. They had established their own independent calendar of religious events. There was rivalry and hatred between the two peoples.

On His way to Jerusalem to offer Himself as a sacrifice for the sins of the world, Christ passed through Samaria. According to verses 52, 53, "He sent messengers before his face: and they went, and entered into a village of the Samaritans, to make ready for him. And they did not receive him, because his face was as though he would go to Jerusalem." Earlier in His ministry our Lord had offered Himself as the water of life to the Samaritans. In His encounter with the woman at the well He had revealed Himself as the Messiah who was to be the Savior of the world. Multitudes in Samaria through the testimony of that woman and through His own testimony believed His word. Read again the fourth chapter of John's gospel. The chapter concludes in what seems to be a note of triumph for many of the Samaritans believed on Him. Now Christ is making His way through that very area where many had believed on Him. But where are those who had professed to believe? Now that Christ is on His way to Jerusalem and needs hospitality for the night, there are none who stand up to identify with Him, who will give Him a night's lodging, food for the body, and rest during the hours of darkness. We can only conclude that those who had heard His word in John 4 and who had believed His word were not willing to commit themselves totally and completely to Him. They had progressed to the place of confidence in His word but had not progressed to the place of commitment to His person. When Christ came into their midst to attract to Himself those who had believed on Him, He found none. The Samaritans rejected Him and did not receive Him because His face was as though He would go to Jerusalem.

What was it that kept these Samaritans from a committal to the Person of Jesus Christ? It was the religious differences between Samaritanism and Judaism. When it came to a question of complete commitment to the Person of Christ, acceptance of and obedience to His word, their old religious forms and practices and prejudices loomed greater than the Person of Christ, and, wonder of wonders, it was religion that kept these people from complete committal to the Person of Christ. So wedded were they to a system, ungodly as it was, they were kept from obedience to the Word of God and to the Person of Christ.

How many there are who could call themselves disciples of Christ today, but they are so engrained in some religious system that denies the Person and work of Jesus Christ that, when it comes to a choice between those forms of religion and the Person of Jesus Christ, they hold to their forms and reject Him. They are not willing to identify themselves with the Word of God and with the Person of Jesus Christ to be known as His disciples. The approval of organized religion means more to them than acceptance by Jesus Christ as a disciple of His. And some who were convinced that He was the Messiah, the Son of God, refused to identify with Him when it meant they had to leave Samaritanism, and the forms and practices of religion to go with Him to Jerusalem. They had accepted His word but would not identify with a person when it involved leaving that which was corrupt and under the judgment of God.

When we come to verse 57, we find one running to volunteer himself as a disciple of Christ: "It came to pass, that, as they went in the way, a certain man said unto him, Lord, I will follow thee whithersoever thou goest." It appears as though the Lord has made one disciple, because this man did not wait to be summoned — he came and offered himself. Yet our Lord, who knows what is in the heart of man, knew that that which motivated this man in his offer of himself as a disciple was not complete commitment and obedience to the Person of Christ. This man was motivated by materialistic desires. The Old Testament made it very clear that, when Messiah comes to reign, He will reign in peace and righteousness; men will beat their swords into plowshares and their spears into pruninghooks. His reign will be a reign of great prosperity and an abundant provision for the material needs for all who are subjects of His kingdom. One who anticipated entrance into the kingdom could anticipate entrance into material prosperity and blessing. This man, focusing attention on that which the Old Testament promised of Messiah's provision for His people, said, "I want to become a disciple of Christ so that I now might enter into the material benefits that He will provide for those who are His." He was not motivated by a love for the Person of Christ. Nor was he motivated by a desire to submit his will to the will of Christ. He was greedy and selfish and materialistic in coming to offer himself as a disciple of Christ.

This man, again, is convinced of the truth of the word but he is not committed to the Person of Christ; he is committed to the pursuit of material wealth. When Christ revealed to him that the "Foxes have holes, and the birds of the air have nests; but the Son of man hath not where to lay his head," the man turned away in disillusionment and discouragement. The time of blessing can come to this earth only after the time of Christ's enthronement as King of kings and Lord of lords. God does not promise material rewards to those who become His and who give themselves completely to the Person of Christ. He may turn a man's material prosperity into poverty that God might teach him the lesson of the sufficiency of Jesus Christ. God might strip away what a man has to show a man where his love actually was so that a man might become a disciple of Christ. We have no promise that our bank accounts will automatically double when we commit ourselves to Him. Christ reminded this man that, as He walked the length and breadth of that land, He had no home to call His own, He was dependent on those who had been moved by His ministry to support His material needs (a group of women from Galilee supplied Him from their material substance). This man was tested as to his submission to the will of Christ, and he turned away, for he wanted the material benefits apart from the submission of his will to the will of Christ.

Christ summoned another in verse 59, and said, "Follow me." This was a call as clear as that which came to Peter or Andrew by Galilee's shores, or to the Apostle Paul on the Damascus Road. The man, knowing what was involved, said, "Lord, suffer me first to go and bury my father. Jesus said unto him, Let the dead bury their dead: but go thou and preach the kingdom of God." Unless we understand this in its setting, we cannot see or understand our Lord's answer to this man. How perfectly reasonable for a man to request to be permitted to go and do the functions of the eldest son in seeing to his father's burial. How unreasonable it seems to demand that this man not do what was expected of the firstborn son. But as we understand the setting, the father had not yet died. He was still hale and hearty. The young man knew that, when his father did die, he would come into his inheritance; and, when he came into his inheritance, he would have that which could sustain him as a disciple of Jesus Christ. What had Christ just said to the one who came and offered himself? He said, ". . . Foxes have holes, and birds of the air have nests, but I have nowhere to lay my head." So, when Christ invited this man to follow Him, a mental process began to go on in his mind: *My father has an inheritance to leave to me and, when my father leaves that inheritance, I will be self-sustaining. Now, since Christ does not have material provisions to make for me, it would be wisest for me if I did not become a disciple until I can support myself; and, after I am independent, then I will become a disciple, completely committed to the Person of Jesus Christ.*

What was this man's problem? He would not or could not trust the Person of Christ to meet his needs as a disciple. The man was self-sufficient, independent, and he did not want to be obligated to Christ. Therefore, he would rather postpone the decision and the commitment to Christ until he did not have to depend upon Christ.

This is one of the major temptations of the age in which we live. Pride demands that we be self-sufficient. Self-sufficiency demands that we can make and pay our own way — that we be dependent on no one. A man's desire to be able to take care of himself often keeps that man from committing himself completely and totally to the Person of Jesus Christ. He refuses to be brought to the place of dependence. Until he is willing to depend on Christ, he cannot be a disciple of Jesus Christ.

A third man came to Christ in verse 61 and said, "Lord, I will follow thee, but let me first go bid them farewell, which are at home in my house. And Jesus said unto him, No man, having put his hand to the plough, and looking back, is fit for the kingdom of God." This man came and offered himself, but first he asked to be excused from immediate discipleship because the home ties had not been broken. The fact that these home ties exist suggests to us that this man recognized the authority of a father that took precedence over the authority of Christ. According to the oriental custom, as long as the father lived, the father was the head of the home. No matter how old the sons became, they were under the authority of their father until the father's death. When this man asked to be permitted to go and bid farewell to them that were at his house, he was saying, "I recognize your authority but the authority of my father takes precedence over your authority and I can't do anything for you until I get my father's permission." This was a recognition of an authority other than the authority of Jesus Christ. Until a man is willing to recognize the absolute authority of Jesus Christ in his life, he is not and cannot be a disciple of Christ.

When we turn to the fourteenth chapter of the gospel of Luke, we find some illustrations of that which the Lord has been teaching in the ninth chapter given to us very briefly in our Lord's parable. In verse 16 we read, "A certain man made a great supper, and bade many: And sent his servant at supper time to say to them that were bidden, Come; for all things are now ready. And they all with one consent began to make excuse. The first said unto him, I have bought a piece of ground, and I must need go and see it; I pray thee have me excused." His business stood between him and the Lord Jesus. "Another said, I have bought five yoke of oxen, and I go to prove them: I pray thee have me excused." Material considerations kept him from the Lord Jesus. "Another said, I have married a wife, therefore I can not come." Excuse follows excuse. Christ demanded absolute submission to His authority, complete devotion to His Person, confidence in His word, trust in His provision, and men excused themselves because they would not commit, could not trust, and did not believe.

The Spirit of God does and right now is looking down into your lives. He is putting a finger on an area of known disobedience. While that known disobedience is there, you have no right to call yourself a disciple, for our Lord demands absolute obedience to His word, to His will as revealed in the Word of God, as a prerequisite to discipleship. When did the servant have the right to give orders to his master? When did the bondslave have a right to question the commands of his Lord? By what right do you who know Jesus Christ as a personal Savior sit in judgment on the Word of God and the will of God when God demands absolute obedience to it? When David found himself in rebellion against the Word of God, there was only one thing he could do. We read of it in Psalm 51 and Psalm 32. He came to confess his disobedience, his rebellion, his lawlessness to God and to place himself in submission to the authority of the Scriptures and to the authority of God. If you find yourself in some area of your life in disobedience to the will and Word of God, David's example should set your course. Let the Word of God reveal, then let the commands of the Word of God be your guide. Recognize that Jesus Christ who saved you has the right to be Master and Lord. This is a prerequisite to discipleship.

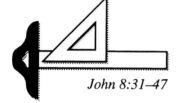

5 The Word and Discipleship

John 8:31–47

The opening verses of John's gospel introduce Jesus Christ as the Light of the world. John speaks of Him and says, "In him was life; and the life was the light of men. And the light shineth in darkness; and the darkness comprehended it not." Because men were dead, Jesus Christ came to give life and the life that He imparted was the Light of men. Men were in ignorance of God and Jesus Christ came to reveal God to men and to dispel that ignorance. The revelation of God to men was the Light of the world. John the Baptizer had the privilege of announcing to men who were in darkness the approach of the sunrise, and John in the first chapter of his gospel relates the ministry of John the Baptizer to the One who was the Light of the world. He said of John that he "came for a witness, to bear witness of the Light, that all men through him might believe. He was not that Light, but was sent to bear witness of that Light. That was the true Light, which lighteth every man that cometh into the world."

Running like a thread through a tapestry, the subject of light weaves its way through the gospel of John. In John 7 where Christ is ministering to the nation in Jerusalem at the Feast of the Tabernacles, we read in verse 14: "Now about the midst of the feast Jesus went up into the temple, and taught. And the Jews marvelled, saying, How knoweth this man letters, having never learned? Jesus answered them, and said, My doctrine is not mine, but his that sent me. If any man will do his will, he shall know of the doctrine [teaching], whether it be of God, or whether I speak of myself."

Jesus Christ came to reveal God to men. This is declared in John 1:18: "No man hath seen God at any time." Therefore, men were in ignorance of God. Men had to depend on a revelation from God, and Christ came to reveal God to men. This revelation which Jesus Christ made was performed through His works and through His words. The works of God were performed by Jesus Christ. The miracles that He performed were obviously the work of God for no man could do those works. As He controlled nature, as He controlled men, as He controlled demons, as He controlled disease and sickness and even death itself, He showed that He was God come in the flesh. That which Christ did in the natural and physical realm was only a picture of what God would do for the needs of men in the spiritual realm. He would remove spiritual blindness and He would make spiritual cripples sound. He would make those who were spiritually dead alive, and He would satisfy those who were spiritually hungry and thirsty. He came to reveal by His works what God would do for men.

The strange thing was that men were not able to transfer from the physical realm to the spiritual realm the truth that Christ sought to reveal. They could see the works of Christ but they could not understand what God was like and what God would do by observing the works. So Christ's works were supplemented by His words. As you read through the gospel, you discover that after a miracle there was an explanation, an application, and an interpretation of the significance of the works that Christ performed. While the gospel of John records seven miracles that reveal the Father, it concentrates on the words that Jesus Christ spoke to explain the works. The revelation made by Christ to men was in His words, and His words became the light that God gave to men, not His works. When Christ stood on that last day of the feast and declared [John 8:12], "I am the light of the world," He was pointing not so much on that occasion to His works as to His words that explained, interpreted and instructed concerning His works. In John 7 when Christ claimed that His doctrine or His teaching came from God, and said to men [verse 17], "If any man will do his will, he shall know of the doctrine, whether it be of God, or whether I speak of myself," He was inviting men to settle the question of His authority. Did He originate His own words or did His words originate from God? If His words were self-generated, they were human words and they were of no more significance than the word of any Jewish rabbi. They were no more significant nor binding than the traditions of men in which the Jews were steeped. But Jesus Christ claimed that His words came from God, and were therefore divinely authoritative and binding. They were true and without error. They were, therefore, to control and guide men in their thinking and in their acting. When Christ (at the time the high priest ascended the ladder in the courtyard and lit the wicks in the great candelabra on that last night of the feast) said, "I am the light of the world," He was saying to men, "I have spoken to you. My words are a revelation of God. They are to be believed and obeyed. I and no other am the Light of the world."

At the conclusion of this great discourse on the Light of the world, according to John 8:30, "As he spake these words, many believed on him." They had heard Him claim that He had come with the Father's message to them, and that He had come to reveal the Father. He had done the works of God and now He has explained the character of the Father in His words with the result that many believed on Him. These would fall into that category of disciples that we have characterized as men who are *convinced*. They had begun as the *curious*. Attracted by His miracles they had given attention to what He had to say. But they were listening to Him as they would to any other innovator, any new teacher or interpreter. Rabbis there were without number and they considered Him another rabbi come to teach. They were curious about what He had to say. But as they have given ear to His teaching, they become convinced that He has truth, that He is truth, and that the word that He speaks has come from God.

The Lord did not deem these to be disciples in the full New Testament concept of the word. Our Lord desired to take those who had progressed from curiosity to conviction beyond that to the place of total and complete *commitment* to the teacher and to His teaching. To those who believed on Him, our Lord had an added word that gives us a test of discipleship. That which the Lord reveals here is vital and crucial to anyone who considers himself a disciple of Jesus Christ in truth. Alas, it is possible to be convinced of the truth of the words that Jesus Christ spoke without being committed to them; and one who is convinced without being committed is not a disciple of Jesus Christ. We remind you once again that we are not dealing with the area of soteriology — we are not dealing with conditions of salvation. Salvation is not made to depend on the human work of committal to Jesus Christ. We are dealing with the area of discipleship.

In John 8:31 Jesus said "to those Jews which believed on him"; that is, who were convinced that His word was truth, "If ye continue in my word, then are ye my disciples indeed." When Christ spoke about continuing in the word, He was not talking about continuing to

believe that what He had to say was truth. The conviction they have
stated is viewed as sufficient and it settles that matter. He is not saying,
if you stay convinced that my word is truth, then you will be my disciples. He is not saying you will cease to be disciples if someone un-
settles your thinking and upsets your conviction so that you begin to
doubt the veracity of the Word of God. This thing of conviction concerning the truth of what Christ stated is viewed as a milestone from
which there will be no retrogression, but it is not the end of the road.
It is not that which makes one a disciple.

The next interpretation pressed upon this word *continue* is that
it means that if we stay in the Word every day, and spend time in
the Word, if we give ourselves to the study of the Word of God, making
it a daily habit to read a portion, making it a habit to study the Word,
then we will be His disciples. Alas, it is true, one may be convinced
of the truth of the Word of God and one may give himself to a detailed study of it and still not be a disciple of Jesus Christ. One can
approach the Word of God with the mind to know truth, to satisfy
an intellectual curiosity. He may give himself to a study in the Word
of God day after day until his mind is saturated with it and still not
be a disciple of Jesus Christ. One becomes a disciple of Jesus Christ
according to this test: when he is controlled in his daily conduct by
the Word that he has learned from Jesus Christ. One may fill his
mind with the Word, and the Word might never penetrate down into
his will so that his will, his actions, his speech, his thoughts are controlled by what the Word of God says. When there is a block between
the mind and the will, one does not satisfy the requirements of verse
31 — "if ye continue in my word, then are ye my disciples indeed."

The word translated *continue* in John 8:31 is the same word that in
John 15:7 is translated *abide*. There Christ said, "If ye abide in me,
and my words abide in you, ye shall ask what ye will, and it shall be
done unto you." What is it to abide in Him and have His Word
abide in us? The word *abide* has in it the idea of drawing from something that which sustains life. The plant is abiding in the ground when
it is so related to its environment, the ground, that it is drawing from
the ground that which nurtures and sustains the life of the plant. The
fish is abiding in the sea, not when it is afloat upside down in the
ocean, but when it is so related to its environment that it is drawing
from that environment sustenance for life. The bird is abiding in the
air when it is drawing from its environment that which sustains its
peculiar kind of life. When there is a break between that living thing
and its environment so that it is not being sustained by it, it is no

longer abiding. A believer is abiding in Christ when his life is being nurtured and sustained by Jesus Christ. A believer is abiding in the Word when he is drawing from the Word that which sustains his life, that which controls his thinking, that which controls his speech, that which controls his actions, that which determines his goals in life, and his habits. When every area and phase of his life is controlled by the Word of God, the individual is living in the Word or abiding in the Word, is dwelling or continuing in the Word.

The men in John 8 had heard. Curiosity caused them to give ear to what Christ said. They had been convinced that what He said was truth, and that His words were Light. They had given assent to the fact that He is Light; they had believed on Him. But Christ said they were not yet disciples. They were not disciples until they put themselves under the authority of the Word and submitted to its teaching, until they were controlled by the Word of God so that they had no thought but what the Word of God teaches, no doctrine but what the Word of God presents, no goals and patterns and desires and ambitions apart from the Word of God. This is what the Word of God says.

This is humiliating to the natural man because the natural man from the time he entered kindergarten was taught to subject everything that was told him to his rational processes. Think it through, analyze it, study it. Accept that which seems reasonable; reject that which seems unreasonable. There is no place for faith in rational thinking. So we have grown up to believe that the highest authority is the mind of man; if not his own mind, then the collective thinking of the intellects of this generation. So we have subjected ourselves to the thinking of men and have deposed that which is Light from its rightful place. Jesus Christ demands the right to control what a man believes; demands the right to control how one who believes in Him acts, and talks. Jesus Christ said, except that relationship between the believer and the authority of the Word of God is real, you cannot be My disciple.

This was a hard thing for Israel to accept. They had been given the law. As a nation, they had received the law from God on Mount Sinai. Rabbis had interpreted the law to tell the nation what it meant and what it required. Gradually they had subverted the law from its authoritative place and they had substituted the teaching of the rabbis. The teaching of the rabbis had been collected, systematized, and codified. They submitted themselves to the traditions of men and in so doing deposed the Word of God from its rightful place of authority and had subjected themselves to the traditions and the doctrines of men. That is why Christ in Matthew 5:20 said, "Except your righteousness shall exceed the righteousness of the Scribes and Pharisees, ye shall in no wise enter in." Why? You cannot be My disciples and derive your teaching from men. It must be from the Word of God. You cannot be My disciples and derive your practices from men; your practices must be practices that are in harmony with the Word of God. Christ repudiated organized religion as being able to make one a disciple.

What that generation faced has its counterpart in what men face today. Men have their tradition, their philosophies, their systems, their religious organizations. These claim to be able to reveal all the truth that is necessary to know about God. They have set aside the Word of God from its rightful place. Will you hear again what Christ said? Except ye abide or continue or submit to the authority of the Word of God over your life, you cannot be My disciple.

This was the foundation of the thinking of the Apostle Paul as revealed in the third chapter of Colossians. The apostle had begun with a reference to the exalted glory of Jesus Christ who is sitting at the right hand of God. He summarized the believer's hope in verse four: "When Christ, who is our life, shall appear, then shall ye also appear with him in glory." He then proceeded to put an obligation on those who have seen and believed the exalted Christ and are possessed of a hope of one day being like Him. He commanded them to put off the old, and [verse 10] put on the new. He then proceeded to spell out what is involved in putting on the new man. Beginning with verse twelve he said, "Put on therefore, as the elect of God, holy and beloved, bowels of mercies, kindness, humbleness of mind, meekness, longsuffering; Forbearing one another, and forgiving one another . . . charity . . . and let the peace of God rule in your hearts." There in verses 12 - 15 the apostle was doing what he did again in the fifth chapter of Galatians when he outlined for us the fruits of the Spirit, that character that the Spirit of God will produce in the child of God when He is permitted to do so.

In verse 16, he revealed how these fruits of the Spirit are manifest in the life of the child of God: "Let the word of Christ dwell in you richly." The apostle says that all of these characteristics of Christ reproduced by the Spirit of God are accomplished in the child of God through the relationship of the child of God to the Word of God, to the control of the child of God by the Word of God. "Let the word of

Christ dwell in you richly." The word *dwell* is an interesting word. It is the word which means to be perfectly at home, to go from place to place, not restricted to the den or the living room. The Word moves in, settles down, and takes over control in the life. The apostle's concept is built on that which Christ taught in the eighth chapter of John's gospel — that one will not become a disciple simply because he assents to the truth of what Christ taught, but he becomes a disciple when he puts himself under the authority of the Word of God and lets the Word of God control his life.

When we go back to the third chapter of the book of Genesis where the record is given of the temptation of Eve, we find that the temptation began with a question about the integrity and authority of the Word of God. Satan came to Eve and said, "Yea, hath God said?" God had given a revelation to Eve. That revelation was in a spoken word. Eve knew and understood that word and recognized an obligation to obey the word. The first temptation was to deny the truth and the authority of the Word of God. Satan works in the lives of believers in exactly the same way today. If he can, he will get us so busy we don't have time for the Word. But he won't object if we insist on giving ourselves to reading the Word, and he won't even be too concerned if we insist on giving ourselves to a careful, detailed study of the Word. Satan realizes that one can quote the Bible from beginning to end, and still be serving him and be safely in his kingdom. Satan doesn't begin to get busy until an individual who reads and studies the Word of God comes to the conviction that his life ought to be changed to conform to the Word of God, and submits to its authority.

If we were to ask if you believe that the Bible is the Word of God, you would assent to the doctrine of the verbal, plenary inspiration of the Scripture. You would confess the authority, integrity, infallibility, and inerrancy of the Word of God. Also if I were to ask if you who believe that the Bible is the Word of God are living by the Word of God, you would admit you are not. How can you call yourself a disciple and not meet the most elementary test? "If ye continue in my word [if the Word of God is the determinative, controlling factor in your life], then are ye my disciples." You have already settled the question: is the Bible the Word of God? Now you need to come face to face with the question of what you are going to do about the Word of God. Are you going to submit to its authority? As God reveals the truth concerning Himself and what He requires of you in the

Word, are you willing to obey it? Are you convinced of the Word of God — or are you committed to it?

The Word of God claims absolute authority over your life. Until you accept the authority of the Word, you have no right to claim to be a disciple of Jesus Christ.

6 The Badge of Discipleship

John 13:20–35

When God appeared to Abraham in Ur of the Chaldees and called him, He not only called him from Ur but He called him to Himself. Abraham was separated from the old life, the old civilization, the old home ties in which he had been brought up, and was separated unto God. Abraham, in an act of faith and in obedience to the command of God, left Ur and began a journey that would ultimately take him into the Land of Promise. After he was separated from Ur and separated unto God, God gave Abraham a sign or badge of his separation. God appeared to Abraham and said, "Thou shalt keep my covenant therefore, thou, and thy seed after thee in their generations. This is my covenant which ye shall keep, between me and you and thy seed after thee; Every man child among you shall be circumcised. And ye shall circumcise the flesh of your foreskin; and it shall be a token of the covenant betwixt me and you. . . . the circumcised man child whose flesh of his foreskin is not circumcised, that soul shall be cut off from his people; he hath broken my covenant" (Gen. 17:9-14).

Abraham was separated from the old life and separated unto God. Circumcision was instituted as a sign that Abraham had been brought into a special relationship with God. It was a sign of the covenant that God had given to Abraham, that Abraham would receive a land and a seed and a blessing, and his people would be blessed and be a blessing to all the peoples of the earth. God, to remind Abraham that Abraham was a separated man, imposed circumcision on him, and on his children after him. Circumcision was required and, if a child were uncircumcised, he was to be cut off from his people. One either received the badge of separation, circumcision, or that one was excluded from fellowship in the commonwealth of Israel. This was an inviolable rule that God laid down: If you are separated unto Me, receive the sign or the badge that I have instituted.

As we trace God's dealing with the nation Israel, we discover in the book of Exodus that God delivered the sons of Abraham from Egyptian bondage by a blood redemption. God liberated them and brought them out into the wilderness. Again, they became a separated people. As Abraham was separated from Ur, so the Israelites were separated from Egypt. As God gave Abraham a sign as his separation from Ur, so at Mt. Sinai God instituted a badge or a sign that the Israelites had been separated from Egypt and were separated to God. This badge was not a badge that they bore in their bodies. In their bodies they already bore the badge of relationship to Abraham. But God instituted a sign that this people, the descendants of Abraham, belonged to God in a unique and special way. The new sign was the observance of the Sabbath Day. In the commandments that God gave to them, He told them that they must "Remember the sabbath day, to keep it holy. Six days shalt thou labour, and do all thy work: But the seventh day is the sabbath of the Lord thy God" (Exod. 20:8-10). It is not until we come to Exodus 31 that we see the significance of the Sabbath. In verse 12 we read: "The Lord spake unto Moses, saying, Speak thou also unto the children of Israel, saying, Verily my sabbaths ye shall keep: for it is a sign between me and you throughout your generations; that ye may know that I am the Lord and doth sanctify [or separate] you." God who separated Abraham from Ur unto Himself has now reached out and separated Abraham's descendants from Egypt unto Himself. As God imposed a sign that Abraham had been separated to God, so God imposed a sign that Abraham's circumcised descendants had been separated to God, and the observance of the Sabbath Day was that sign of sanctification or separation that God gave to the nation Israel.

God was very specific about this sign, as specific and detailed about the sign of the Sabbath as He was about circumcision back in Genesis 17. In Exodus 31:14 God said: "Ye shall keep the sabbath therefore; for it is holy unto you: every one that defileth it shall surely be put to death: for whosoever doeth any work therein, that soul shall be cut off from his people." Verse 16: "Wherefore the children of Israel shall keep the sabbath, to observe the sabbath throughout their generations, for a perpetual covenant. It is a sign between me and the children of Israel for ever." It is stated and repeated that the individual who did not observe the sign of separation should be cut off from fellowship in the nation Israel. As the uncircumcised child was to be excluded because he did not have the badge, so the one who did not observe the Sabbath in Israel was to be cut off because he did not keep the sign of separation unto God.

Now Israel throughout their generations from the time of Abraham and from the time of Sinai observed these two signs. Every male descendant of Abraham was circumcised as a sign that Abraham and Abraham's people had been chosen by God as His own peculiar people; and they observed the Sabbath Day as a sign that as a nation they had been separated from Egypt and were separated to God. Right on down to the time of the coming of Israel's Messiah, the Lord Jesus Christ, these two badges had been recognized and observed in the nation Israel.

It is not until the ministry of John the Baptist that there is mention of another identifying sign in the nation Israel. In the first chapter of John's gospel, there is reference to a new badge, a new identifying sign that is being presented to the nation Israel. We read in John 1:26: "John answered them, saying, I baptize you with water: but there standeth one among you, whom ye know not; He it is, who coming after me is preferred before me, whose shoe's latchet I am not worthy to unloose. These things were done in Bethabara beyond Jordan, where John was baptizing."

John's ministry was new and unique. He was gathering together a group of people who professed their personal faith in the fulfillment of the promises of the Old Testament Word of God. They were a people who believed that God would send the Messiah to redeem and reign. Hearing John's message that the Messiah was about to put in His appearance, they believed that John was a prophet with a message from God. Then John offered them a new identifying sign. It was the sign of water baptism. Those who believed that John was a heaven-sent prophet with a message from God and who believed his message accepted this new identifying sign. They had been circumcised because they were Abraham's seed. They observed the Sabbath Day because they were a part of a redeemed nation, separated from the nations of the earth. Now they received a third identifying sign, the sign of baptism, a sign that they believed that God was about to send the Redeemer who would reign over Israel.

So Israel throughout their history had been introduced to these three identifying signs of three great works of God: the call of Abraham, the redemption of Israel from Egypt, and the sending of Messiah into the world.

Moving into the thirteenth chapter of the gospel of John, we find our Lord taking a small group of men apart into an upper room. They are men who had been circumcised; they are men who throughout their lives had observed the Sabbath Day; they are men, as far as we understand, who had received the identifying sign of John's baptism signifying that they believed that God was about to send the Messiah to redeem them. Now our Lord speaks to them in John 13:34, 35: "A new commandment I give unto you." The new commandment was in contrast to an old commandment. The old commandment: be circumcised, observe the Sabbath Day, be baptized with John's baptism as identifying signs of relationship to the purpose of God and the person of the Redeemer. Now, our Lord says, I am sweeping aside those identifying signs that God gave to Israel; I am supplementing circumcision and Sabbath observance and water baptism by John with a new identifying sign that you are separated to Me. A new commandment, a new identifying sign I give unto you: "That ye love one another; as I have loved you, that ye also love one another. By this shall all men know that ye are my disciples, if ye have love one for another." The love of believer for believer was to be the identifying sign that one was a true disciple of Jesus Christ. As one would never have been recognized as a child of Abraham without circumcision but would have been cut off; and as one would never have been recognized as an Israelite who did not observe the sign of the Sabbath but would have been cut off; and as one would not have been counted a disciple of John who rejected John's baptism but would have been excluded, so our Lord said, you cannot be My disciple apart from the observance of this sign. Love one another.

The love that Christ demanded as the sign of relationship to Him, the sign of discipleship, was the sign that only the Spirit of God could produce. A man could impose circumcision on his son. A father could require Sabbath observance in his household. Only the Spirit of God can produce love for another believer. That is why love for one another is an indisputable proof that one is a disciple of Jesus Christ.

"By this shall all men know that ye are my disciples." Underline that word *my*. Do you want to prove you are a disciple of Abraham? Produce evidence of circumcision. Do you want to prove you are a disciple of Moses? Observe the Sabbath. Do you want to prove you are a disciple of John? Be baptized. But if you want to prove that you are *My* disciple, then Jesus says, do it by loving one another.

In John 14:23 our Lord reminds those upon whom this requirement was made that they have received the Father's love. "Jesus answered and said unto him, If a man love me, he will keep my words: and my Father will love him, and we will come unto him, and make our abode with him." If we may paraphrase this, our Lord is saying that if a man receives Him as personal Saviour, believes on Him to the salvation of his soul, the Father will love him, and the Father and I will come unto him and make our abode with him. Here our Lord is speaking of the intimacy into which the child of God is brought with his heavenly Father the moment he receives Christ as his personal Saviour. The love of God has been shed abroad on the world. That love was manifested in the giving of Jesus Christ to be the Saviour of the world. But men do not enter into the benefits of the love of God until they personally receive Jesus Christ as Saviour. That love that was poured out upon the world becomes the personal possession of the believer in Jesus Christ. The Father not only loves him, but because the Father loves him He moves in and dwells with him. Two people who are deeply and genuinely in love want to spend time together, and every separation is painful. The Father will not be separated from the objects of His affection. He comes and dwells with them and makes His abode with them. So, when our Lord says that the badge of true discipleship is that we love one another, He is basing it on the personal reception of Christ and experience of the love of God for him.

In John 15:9 He gives a commandment based on the truth of 14:23 that we have received the love of God. The Lord says, "As the Father hath loved me, so have I loved you: continue ye in my love." The word *continue* in verse nine is the same word translated *abide* in verse four. It is that truth which we have emphasized previously that one abides in Christ when he draws from Christ that which sustains every facet of his life. One abides in the love of God when he is saturated with, nourished, motivated and controlled by the love of God for him. Our Lord is not focusing attention upon our vacillating love for God but on the constancy of His love for us. We abide in His love when we draw from this love that which sustains every facet of life — our mind saturated with the love of God, our affections controlled by the love of God, our wills moved and dominated by the love that God has for us. So Christ in developing this teaching reminds us in 14:23 that we have received the Father's love and now we can get our roots deep in that love of God, and as a plant draws from its native soil that which sustains it, so we through our spiritual roots in the love of God are nourished and satisfied and grow because of the constancy of God's love for us.

Then in verses 12 and 13 He says, "This is my commandment, That ye love one another, as I have loved you. Greater love hath no man than this, that a man lay down his life for his friends [the objects of his affection]." Our Lord in the progression of thought has shown us that, when we are rooted and grounded in the love of God, we will manifest that love one to another. "This is my commandment, That ye love one another, as I have loved you."

Our Lord was deeply concerned that His disciples should manifest the badge of discipleship. When He went to the Father in His High Priestly prayer in John 17, while the prayer begins with His own need, a prayer for His resurrection and glorification, He soon moves on in His prayer to pray for the believers' protection, and, working up to the climax, He prays in verse 21, "That they all may be one." In verse 26 He says, "I have declared unto them [the disciples] thy name, and I will declare it: that the love wherewith thou hast loved me may be in them." Will you notice that, as far as Scripture records it, the last prayer our Lord prayed for believers was a prayer that they might manifest the badge of discipleship that He had given them? "Hereby shall all men know that ye are my disciples, if ye have love one to another," and "I have declared unto them thy name, and will declare it: that the love wherewith thou hast loved me may be in them."

It seems in this prayer as though our Lord's concern with the cross pales into insignificance in His concern that those who name the name of Christ should manifest the badge of discipleship that He has appointed to them.

The love about which Christ is speaking is a concern for the well-being of the object of one's affections. It is an occupation with that individual instead of an occupation with one's self. It is a care for the welfare of that person, a desire to see that his needs are met whether they be physical, material, mental, emotional, or spiritual. To be so occupied with another with the love of Christ is the badge of discipleship. The badge of a disciple of Satan is that he is occupied with himself. The badge of a disciple of Jesus Christ is that he is occupied with those whom Jesus Christ loves.

This formed the basis for Paul's great exhortation to the Ephesians when he prayed, in Ephesians 3:18, 19: That ye "may be able to comprehend with all saints what is the breadth, and length, and depth, and height; And to know the love of Christ, which passeth knowledge."

After he had given the great doctrinal truths, Paul prayed that they might experientially enter into the love of Christ. Why this occupation with the love of Christ? So that these Ephesian believers might manifest the badge of discipleship. He continues in 4:2, 3: "With all lowliness and meekness, with longsuffering, forbearing one another in love; Endeavouring to keep the unity of the Spirit in the bond of peace." Verses 30, 31: "And grieve not the holy Spirit of God, whereby ye are sealed unto the day of redemption. Let all bitterness, and wrath, and anger, and clamour, and evil speaking, be put away from you, with all malice." These are all sins against brothers, sins against love. He continues, "Be ye kind one to another, tenderhearted [or loving], forgiving one another, even as God for Christ's sake hath forgiven you." Do you see the burden of the apostle? I want you to know the love of Christ (3:19) in order that you might manifest the love of Christ to other believers, and put away all sins against love that you might bear the badge that you are true disciples of Jesus Christ (4: 30-32).

I see this again in Hebrews 12:15 in that great section on faith and the application of faith in daily conduct: "Looking diligently lest any man fail of the grace of God; lest any root of bitterness springing up trouble you." The root of bitterness would be any sin against love; any failure to manifest the badge of true discipleship toward another believer would mean that many would be defiled. The apostle is viewing an assembly of believers. One believer is at variance with another. This bitterness, this failure to manifest the badge of true discipleship, that exists between the two would begin to spread like a canker until it had corrupted the whole assembly. When unbelievers watched that assembly of believers and saw discord and strife and bitterness and jealousy, they completely lost any testimony to Jesus Christ in that whole assembly of believers. This is the great burden of the Apostle John who had sat with our Lord in the upper room and heard His words, as he writes his first epistle. In chapter after chapter, John drives this great truth home to those who lived in Ephesus that they were responsible to love one another.

The society in which we live has made it extremely difficult for us today to manifest the badge of true discipleship. The world has confused love of Christ with sex. Having given itself over to immorality and perversion, the world cannot understand love of the brethren. If a man manifests the love of God to another man, he is suspect. And if a brother manifests love to a sister in Christ, he is suspected of having immoral motives. Such is the perversion of the world. Fearing the perversion in which we live, we have failed to manifest the badge of discipleship which Jesus Christ said is the one sign that we are His disciples.

Have you wondered why Paul closes epistle after epistle with the words, "Greet one another with a holy kiss"? Paul recognized that there was only one sign that one was a true disciple of Jesus Christ, and that was that he loved the other. That love was not concealed, not hinted at, not intimated — it was openly expressed. When someone is flat on his back, completely helpless, we show care or concern or interest in him. Why, when someone is strong and healthy, can't we manifest love of Christ for him, showing care, interest, concern for his physical, mental, emotional, spiritual well-being?

Something is wrong if you have to look at your pastor and say, I wonder if he loves his flock. If the pastor has to look at the flock and say, "I wonder if the sheep love their pastor," something is wrong. When a believer has to look at another believer and question his love, something is wrong. Christ didn't say you are My disciples if you join a church; you are My disciples if you are baptized; you are My disciples if you attend home Bible classes. He said you are My disciples if you manifest love one to another.

Our formal greeting is: "How do you do?" Technically that means, I want you to tell me how you are, what your needs are, for I am concerned. If someone takes you literally and begins to tell you, you are bored to tears because you don't care that much. We have reduced what should be a genuine proof of discipleship to a mere formality which we don't expect to be answered.

God has not constituted believers to stand alone. God has provided for the fellowship of the saints. That fellowship unites believer with believer so that there might be in this mutual love strength, support, and encouragement. God will not accept adherence to the truths of the fundamentals of the Word as a substitute for adherence to the one badge He has given that one is a disciple of Jesus Christ. "Hereby shall all men know that ye are my disciples, if ye have love one for another." You may be a believer without manifesting love but you cannot be a true disciple without that badge that was given as a sign that you have received His love.

7 Authority and Discipleship

Luke 14:16–27

Our Lord offered Himself to the nation Israel as a Saviour and a King. He demanded that those who believed on Him should submit to the authority of His Word and of His Person. His invitation to the nation is summarized in Matthew 11:28, "Come unto me, all ye that labour and are heavy laden, and I will give you rest." *Come unto me.* This is believing. That required of those who come to Him is laid down in verses 29 and 30, "Take my yoke upon you, and learn of me; for I am meek and lowly in heart: and ye shall find rest unto your souls. For my yoke is easy, and my burden is light." One did not become a disciple of Jesus Christ until he had submitted to the authority of Christ, until he had taken Christ's yoke upon him.

That nation to whom Christ offered Himself as a Saviour and Sovereign understood full well both the invitation, "Come unto me," and the requirement, "take my yoke upon you." In the fourteenth chapter of Luke's gospel (the parable of the great supper), our Lord explained the response of the nation to His invitation. We read in verse 16: "A certain man made a great supper, and bade many: And sent his servant at supper time to say to them that were bidden, Come; for all things are now ready." Throughout the prophetic Scriptures, the figure of a supper, or a banquet, was used to describe the blessings, the glories, the joys, the fellowship of Messiah's kingdom. In this parable our Lord likened Himself to a man who provided a banquet for his friends. He sent out the word that the banquet to which they had previously been bidden was ready and they were to come and enjoy what they had been promised. Those who had been bidden realized that to come to him meant to submit to his authority. The parable continues in Luke 14:18, "They all with one consent began to make excuse."

The nation that had been bidden rejected His invitation. Those who had been invited to become His disciples had repudiated His call. They deemed the cost to be more than they were willing to assume. In verse 25, to conclude the teaching of this parable, our Lord turned to the great multitude and said to them, "If any man come to me, and hate not his father, and mother, and wife, and children, and brethren, and sisters, yea, and his own life also, he cannot be my disciple. And whosoever doth not bear his cross, and come after me, cannot be my disciple." Our Lord was laying down requirements for discipleship, and in this passage He made it clear that the cost of discipleship was hatred of father and mother and wife and children and brethren and sisters and, yea, his own life; for, until one hates those to whom he has the closest natural ties, our Lord says, he cannot be My disciple.

This seems to involve us in a contradiction, for the family relationship was a divine institution. The marriage relationship had been instituted by God in the Garden of Eden. The ties that bind husband to wife and children to parents were established by God at the time of the creation of the human race. How, then, can Christ make demands upon a man that countermands the oldest established order that God has instituted? How can Christ ask a man to hate his father and mother when the law of the home established by God is that children should obey their parents in the Lord? How can a man be called upon to hate his wife when the Apostle Paul, in Ephesians 5:22 commands that a man love his wife as Christ loved the church? How can Christ ask a wife to set aside the authority of her husband to become a disciple of Christ when the Apostle Paul in Ephesians 5:20 demands that a wife submit to the authority of her husband? How can a man set aside his own life to become a disciple of Jesus Christ? God has instituted certain spheres of authority. In the home God has constituted the husband, the father, as the head of the home. Wife and children are subject to that authority by divine appointment and the home is not a home according to the pattern of God until the relationships within the home conform to God's pattern for that home. Yet Christ demands hatred in place of love.

According to Jewish idiom and usage, while love and hatred on occasion have to do with the realm of the emotions, frequently they have to do with the area of the will. That to which a man surrenders himself he is said to love, and that which attempts to gain mastery over him which he repudiates he is said to hate. Christ in Luke 14:26 is not dealing with the area of the emotions but rather the area of the submission of the will. He is not dealing with affections; he rather is dealing with the area of authority in a man's life.

To see this more clearly, turn back to Malachi 1:2, 3. God affirms through the prophet to the nation Israel, "I have loved you, saith the Lord. Yet ye say, Wherein hast thou loved us?" God affirmed His love for Israel. What is the love about which He is speaking? Wherein do we see God's love for Israel? The answer comes at the end of verse 2: "Was not Esau Jacob's brother? saith the Lord: yet I loved Jacob, and I hated Esau."

To understand this, it is necessary to go back in Israel's history to the record given in the book of Genesis. Twin boys were born to Isaac. While these boys were still in their mother's womb, God had said that He appointed Jacob as the heir of Isaac through whom His covenant promises would be fulfilled. By choosing Jacob to be the heir in the line of Isaac, He set Esau aside. This was not a matter of the affections; this was not a matter of the emotions. This was a matter of the will of God in which God sovereignly purposed to fulfill His promise made to Abraham and to Isaac through Jacob rather than through Esau. Esau became the father of a great race as Jacob became the father of a great race. But God's purpose rested in God's sovereign choice, the choice of Jacob rather than Esau.

When Malachi was asked the question, "Wherein did God love us?" the reply through the prophet was that God loved and this love was demonstrated by an act of His will in which He sovereignly set aside the firstborn and put the younger in the place of preeminence. This same truth is emphasized in the ninth chapter of Romans when the apostle quotes Malachi, and in verse 13 says, "Jacob have I loved, but Esau have I hated." This is explained in verse 11: "(The children being not yet born, neither having done any good or evil, that the purpose of God according to election might stand, not of works, but of him that calleth;) It was said unto her, The elder shall serve the younger." Will you notice that the love for Jacob in verse 13 is related to that which God purposed in verse 11?

When a Jewish father adopted a child into his family (because no children had been born to him and his wife), and selected one son from a number of children, that father was said to have loved the one whom he adopted, and he hated the rest whom he did not choose for adoption. This was not an emotional response to those whom he did not adopt — no anger, malice, wrath or bitterness against those whom he did not put into his family. Love had to do with putting one into his family as his heir. This was the choice of his will. That father, I repeat, was said to have loved the one chosen and hated the ones that were passed over. When Christ in Luke 14:26 asked His disciples to hate, He was not dealing so much with the affections as with the choice of the will; a decision as to whose authority one will accept. Even though God has instituted authority in the home, that authority itself is subject to the authority of God. The father's authority over his children is a derived authority which is subject to the authority of God. The wife who submits herself to the authority of her husband, submits herself in the Lord recognizing that it is the Lord's authority that has been given to her husband to which she submits. But it is possible for one to discount the supreme authority that belongs to Jesus Christ and to substitute a lesser authority than the authority of Christ. If one submits to any constituted authority that is not itself subject to the authority of Christ, one is not subject to Christ and, therefore, he is not a disciple of Jesus Christ.

May we paraphrase Luke 14:26 this way? Jesus says, If a man hears My invitation and comes to Me and is not willing to set aside every authority which would seek to exercise its authority over him and submit absolutely and finally to My authority, he cannot be My disciple. Our Lord is dealing here with a question of authority. He is dealing with the question of the right to rule, the question of the one to whom and with whom we are yoked. No natural tie is a substitute for being yoked to Jesus Christ. Until one recognizes that he must be yoked to Jesus Christ, he is not a disciple of Jesus Christ.

Our Lord, in the parable that preceded this statement, listed three excuses which men were giving for repudiating His authority. The three who made personal excuses are representative of three kinds of people and three excuses that were being given as to why a man should not submit to the authority of Christ and His Word to become His disciple. The invitation had gone out (verse 17), "Come; for all things are now ready." Now, the excuses began to roll in. The first said unto Him, "I have bought a piece of ground, and I must needs go and see it: I pray thee have me excused." The piece of ground which the man had just purchased represented his material possessions, that in which he placed great value in this life. The man was secular, materialistic; he viewed his successes by that which he could accumulate and he deemed himself to have been a success because he was able to purchase a piece of property. His whole interest, his whole life was given over to that material thing which he had been able to accumulate. He desired to exercise authority over that material thing and, therefore, he repudiated the authority of Christ over him in order that he might exercise independent authority over those material things. That to which the man gave attention and devotion had become his master; it had become his lord. Discipleship to Christ involves the Lordship of Christ. A man cannot be dominated by material things and submissive to the absolute Lordship of Jesus Christ at the same time.

A man may be eminently successful in the business world and be blessed of God with material things and still be a disciple of Jesus Christ, but, when a man gives himself to be a servant of material things, he has repudiated the right of Jesus Christ to be his Master and he has become the disciple of material things and not the disciple of Jesus Christ.

Multitudes of men today know that Jesus Christ is inviting them to become His disciples, to submit to His authority in every area of their lives — but material things have so gripped them that they have so become the servants of material things that they have become the prisoners of them. When money becomes an end in itself, it prevents one from being a disciple of Jesus Christ. It is only when money can be a means to an end that one can have material things and be a disciple of Jesus Christ.

The second man made his excuse. He said, "I have bought five yoke of oxen, and I go to prove them. I pray thee have me excused." No one would be so foolish as to invest the large sum necessary to purchase five yoke of oxen without first having tried them out. This man was not going to see if he had made a good investment. He had set himself up in business. A man can work only one yoke of oxen himself. He cannot possibly work two yoke of oxen at the same time, or five yoke of oxen. To work five yoke of oxen it means there have to be at least four other drivers; there were probably five others so that he could be the supervisor of the five. The man had established himself in business. He was different from the first, for in the first we are concerned with a man who had made a material investment; he had material wealth, and he was enjoying that wealth, and that wealth had become a barrier between him and discipleship with Jesus Christ. This second man was a man who did not yet have it made. But he is on his way in the business world and now he was going to give himself completely to business so he could become a success in it.

Your business life can stand between you and becoming a disciple of Jesus Christ. Your business can demand your effort, your strength, your time, your energy so that you have no time for the Lord Jesus Christ. Business today does not demand eight to five o'clock from a man — it demands twenty-four hours a day. So giving yourself to business you are becoming a servant of business, not a servant of Jesus Christ. You are a disciple of business, not a disciple of Jesus Christ. Men are going to have to make a decision as to whether they become what this world calls a successful business man or a servant of Jesus Christ.

The third man said, "I have married a wife, and therefore I can not come." This man had availed himself of that which God, according to the Word of God, has provided for the welfare of man. Marriage is a divine provision for man's physical, mental, and emotional needs. This man had taken that which is a gift of God, and had substituted that for the rightful place that Jesus Christ demands if a man is to be a disciple. God has not changed His law of marriage. God still demands that a husband love his wife as Christ loved the church. But this man had taken God's blessing and made that the thing he served above everything else, and he had repudiated Christ's absolute right to rule him. It was out of this third excuse I think that our Lord's application in verse 26 came as He said, "If any man come to me [respond to my invitation], and hate not his father, and mother, and wife, and children, and brethren, and sisters, yea, and his own life also, he cannot be my disciple." If a man responds to My invitation and does not put Me above everyone or everything that demands submission, whether it be material possessions, business, profession, whether it be relationships in the home, he cannot be My disciple.

Perhaps this last excuse is the hardest to cope with because of the ties with which God binds parents to children, husbands to wives, according to the Word of God. Here is an area in which there is real danger. We as parents want the best for our children. We want them to go to the best schools, discounting the fact that the school to which we are sending our young people is a godless, immoral center of blatant unbelief. Because of the standing it will give them, we send them anyway for the benefits and the prestige that school will give to our children. Then we wonder why they come out from that environment corrupted and tainted by it. Desiring that our children have social graces, we send them to dancing school to attain them — and wonder why they get into trouble after the dance. We pay their way to get on the world's merry-go-round then wonder why they fall off when the merry-go-round gets going too fast. Wanting so much for our children, we haven't realized that our relationship to them must be governed first of all by our relationship to Jesus Christ.

Some time ago a mother made an appointment and came to my office. She walked in the door and broke into tears before she could even sit down. I waited for her to tell me the tragedy that had come to her. She told me that she had received a letter from her college daughter in which the daughter told her she had volunteered to go to the mission field and had written to tell her parents about it. It was the worst tragedy that those parents had ever experienced. The mother reminded me of all that they had invested in the daughter's education, and all the things they had given the daughter, and the good marriage they desired for her. Now she was throwing it all away. Such an attitude is not uncommon.

Remember that unless you put Jesus Christ above father, mother, wife and children, and brothers, and sisters, yea, even your own life, you cannot be His disciple. According to the original law of marriage laid down in the Garden of Eden, God said a man should leave his father and mother and cleave unto his wife. Leaving father and mother to cleave unto the wife did not mean that the affection that a child had for his parents was repudiated or that love turned to hatred, but it did mean that one was leaving one sphere of authority to establish a new sphere of authority. Christ said that in family relationships, in social relationships, in business relationships, until you recognize the absolute authority of Jesus Christ over that area of your life, you are not His disciple.

Once again in the light of that which Christ has required, many of us would have to come to God and confess that, while we have believed to the saving of our souls, we have not accepted His authority in our business lives, over our material possessions, over our family, over our children. We want our own will in our own way — not God's will and God's way. We would have to confess that, while we are believers, we are not disciples. "Come unto me" — His invitation; "take my yoke upon you," or submit to My authority — the condition. Are you a disciple of Jesus Christ?

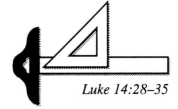

8 Sacrifice and Discipleship

Luke 14:28–35

Can one be a thief and a disciple of Jesus Christ? Can one be an embezzler and a disciple of Jesus Christ at the same time? I am sure your answer would be, "No." On the basis of your answer, I would say I am addressing men and women and young people who are not disciples of Jesus Christ. For while I would not accuse you of being thieves, I accuse you of being embezzlers.

A thief is a man who takes that which is not rightfully his and uses it for his own ends. An embezzler is more despicable than a thief in that the embezzler takes that which has been committed to his trust, over which he has supervision, and misappropriates it, misdirects it, and uses it for ends other than that for which it was entrusted to him. In the light of the teaching of the Word of God, we stand guilty of embezzlement. We have taken that which God has entrusted to us and we have treated it as though it were our own rather than His. We have used if for our own ends, and Jesus Christ says such a man is not a disciple of His.

In discussing the question of discipleship in Luke 14:33 Christ said, "Whosoever he be of you that forsaketh not all that he hath, he cannot be my disciple." Unless one forsakes all that he has, he is not a disciple. Jesus Christ is interested in making embezzlers into disciples. But He does not make an embezzler a disciple. By virtue of the fact that God created this earth and all that is within it, all things belong to Him. No man can contest God's absolute right to this universe because He made it by the Word of His mouth. "All things were created by him, and for him" (Col. 1:16). At the time of the creation of man, this earth was subjected to the authority of man. Man received a right to rule as God's representative over that which God possessed. In giving the right to man, God did not surrender His rights but God did expect man to recognize His rights to all things that He had created.

Early in human history men recognized that God owned all things because they paid tithes to God. Long before the giving of the law, Abraham paid tithes to Melchizedek (Gen. 14:20). Abraham paid tithes to Melchizedek because Abraham recognized that Melchizedek was a priest of the Most High God, a mediator between God and himself. Further, he paid tithes not to honor Melchizedek but to honor the God whom Melchizedek served. The payment of the tithe was a recognition that all Abraham had gained in the conquest of Chedorlaomer was not rightfully his, it was rightfully God's. A victory in battle brought Abraham great spoils but the conquest did not give Abraham title-deed to the spoils, for they belonged to God. God, because of Abraham's conquest, did not relinquish His right to all that He had created. Abraham paid tithes as a recognition that all that had been given to him came from God, as a trust from God, and that ownership belonged to God.

The law of the tithe was developed in great detail in the law given to Israel through Moses on Mt. Sinai. From the Old Testament revelation the principle of the tithe as a recognition of God's ownership of all things is familiar to us. What we are not familiar with from a cursory study of the Old Testament, perhaps, is how extensive the tithe was, nor how great the burden of taxation God placed upon the Israelites. As we read through the law we discover that there was not one tithe, but rather three separate tithes that God demanded of the children of Israel.

The first tithe is described in Numbers 18:21 - 24: "Behold, I have given the children of Levi all the tenth in Israel for an inheritance, for their service which they serve, even the service of the tabernacle of the congregation. But the tithes of the children of Israel, which they offer as an heave-offering unto the Lord, I have given to the Levites to inherit: therefore I have said unto them, Among the children of Israel they shall have no inheritance." This tithe is further explained in Leviticus 27:30-34: "All the tithe of the land, whether of the seed of the land, or of the fruit of the tree, is the Lord's: it is holy unto the Lord. And if a man will at all redeem aught of his tithes, he shall add thereto the fifth part thereof. And concerning the tithe of the herd, or of the flock, even of whatsoever passeth under the rod, the tenth shall be holy unto the Lord. He shall not search whether it be good or bad, neither shall he change it: and if he change it at all, then both it and the change thereof shall be holy; it shall not be redeemed."

These two passages describe the first tithe, the tithe that was given to the Levites. This tithe was recognized as the Lord's tithe. It was a tithe that was given to the Levites to support them in their ministry and to support the Tabernacle in its ministry. The Tithe was a tithe of all that grew on the land. It was also a tithe of all the flocks and the herds. This tithe was obligatory. It was a recognition that all that they had came from the Lord and they gave the tithe to the Lord and to the Levites in recognition that all things belonged to God.

The second tithe is described in the book of Deuteronomy. As the first tithe was an annual tithe, so this second tithe was an annual tithe. It was a tithe to make it possible for the Israelites to observe the annual feasts to Jehovah. Deuteronomy 14:22-26 tells us: "Thou shalt truly tithe all the increase of thy seed, that the field bringeth forth year by year. And thou shalt eat before the Lord thy God, in the place which he shall choose to place his name there, the tithe of thy corn, of thy wine, and of thine oil, and the firstlings of thy herds and of thy flocks; that thou mayest learn to fear the Lord thy God always. And if the way be too long for thee, so that thou art not able to carry it; or if the place be too far from thee, which the Lord thy God shall choose to set his name there, when the Lord thy God hath blessed thee: Then shalt thou turn it into money, and bind up the money in thine hand, and shalt go unto the place which the Lord thy God shall choose: And thou shalt bestow that money for whatsoever thy soul lusteth after, for oxen, or for sheep, or for wine, or for strong drink, or for whatsoever thy soul desireth: and thou shalt eat there before the Lord thy God, and thou shalt rejoice, thou, and thine household."

God had instituted seven feasts which the children of Israel were to observe every year. These feasts entailed the expenditure of money to provide the animals, the fruits, the nuts, the wines, all that was necessary to observe them. In order that every Israelite might have the wherewithal to observe the feasts as He had commanded, God said a man must set apart a second tithe which either he could keep as goods or could convert to money so that if, for instance, he had to travel to Jerusalem to observe the Passover, he would have the money to purchase all that was necessary for the Passover Feast when he got to

Jerusalem. So that no man could neglect his service to God on the plea of poverty, God required the individual to set aside this second tithe. That is twenty percent which each year had to be dedicated to God.

But that is not all. Look at Deuteronomy 14:28, 29. Here we find a tithe that was assessed every third year for the children of Israel. "At the end of three years thou shalt bring forth all the tithes of thine increase the same year, and shalt lay it up within thy gates: And the Levite (because he hath no part nor inheritance with thee,) and the stranger, and the fatherless, and the widow, which are within thy gates, shall come, and shall eat and be satisfied; that the Lord thy God may bless thee in all the work of thine hands which thou doest." This third tithe was the tithe for the poor. Every third year the children of Israel were to set aside the third tithe in a separate fund so that the poor, the indigent, the widows, the orphans, might be provided for in the land of Israel. This was divine social security, if you please, for which God assessed the third tithe.

For the first and second years, the children of Israel had to give God twenty percent, the third year the tax was raised to thirty percent, but that was not the end. You will remember that God required offerings over and above the tithe. These offerings were voluntary offerings in which an individual recognized God's goodnesses and mercies to him, and he gave over and above that which God required as a thank offering to God for what God had given to him. The Israelite who sought to live according to the command of the Mosaic Law gave God at least a third of his annual income. As stringent as these laws were, we find through Israel's history down to the time of the Babylonian captivity that the children of Israel obeyed without question. No matter how far from God their hearts were, they still observed the law of the tithes. The prophets who ministered to them, while they had to condemn them for many moral and social sins, did not call them to question concerning the matter of giving, for they recognized that God required the tithes because all things belonged to God and all they had came from Him.

It is not until the prophecy of Malachi after the Babylonian captivity that we find the children of Israel neglecting the law of the tithe. In Malachi 3:7, 8, God said, "Even from the days of your fathers ye are gone away from mine ordinances, and have not kept them. Return unto me, and I will return unto you, saith the Lord of Hosts. But ye said, Wherein shall we return? Will a man rob God? Yet ye have robbed me. But ye say, Wherein have we robbed thee?" And the answer comes: "In tithes and offerings." The result of withholding the tithes and the offerings from God was that they were "cursed with a curse: for ye have robbed me, even this whole nation. Bring ye all the tithes [the tithes for the Levites and the Temple, the tithe for the annual feast, the tithe for the poor — bring ye all the tithes] into the storehouse, that there may be meat in my house, and prove me now herewith, saith the Lord of hosts, if I will not open you the windows of heaven, and pour you out a blessing, that there shalt not be room enough to receive it. And I will rebuke the devourer for your sakes, and he shalt not destroy the fruits of your ground; neither shall your vine cast her fruit before the time in the field, saith the Lord of hosts. And all nations shall call you blessed; for ye shall be a delightsome land, saith the Lord of hosts."

We find the heart of the matter in verse 13. They had withheld their tithes from God because they renounced God's right to rule over them. This withholding was a repudiation that they belonged to God and of the fact that all they had came from God. God saw through the actual act of embezzling from Him to the heart that caused them to embezzle. God said they had repudiated Him and renounced His authority over them, and the outward evidence of that was that they had withheld their tithes from Him.

When we turn to the New Testament, we find that the children of Israel were again scrupulously observing the law of the tithe. It was most difficult for them to do so, for in addition to the thirty percent that they had to pay in tithes to Israel, they must add the heavy burden of taxation that the Romans imposed upon the nation as a conquered people. That grievous weight of Roman taxation would seem to give them cause to renounce their responsibility to God, but in Matthew 23: 23 our Lord acknowledges the fact that the Pharisees paid tithes of mint and anise and cummin. They not only tithed the grains which could easily be measured in a bushel, they tithed the leaves that came from the plants that would have spiced their food. Now the question comes to those who have heard Jesus Christ offer Himself as a King and as a Saviour as to how much they should give to Him? They had heard our Lord say, "Come unto me, all ye that labour and are heavy laden, and I will give you rest." The question comes to the minds of His would-be disciples, "Does His rest mean rest from taxation? Does His rest mean rest from the responsibility of giving a third of what we earn to God?" So our Lord in Luke 14:33 is dealing with the question of discipleship and material things. He says, "Whosoever he be of you who forsaketh not all that he hath, he cannot be my disciple." Our Lord was not asking for the first tithe, nor was He adding the second annual tithe and demanding twenty percent as the basis of discipleship, nor did He require the tithe for the poor assessed every third year, demanding thirty percent. He did not add together the tithes that Israel paid to God plus the taxes they paid to the Roman government and say that total was required of a disciple. Our Lord said they could not be His disciples until they acknowledged His absolute right to every penny they possessed.

To illustrate this our Lord used two brief parables. He told the parable of a man intending to build a tower: he sits down first and counts the cost, whether he has sufficient to finish it. In the second parable Jesus told of a king who was prepared to go to war and he consulted whether he would be able with ten thousand to meet him that came against him with twenty thousand. If we understand these parables correctly, our Lord was not dealing with the amount that the man has. He was dealing with the amount that the man was willing to commit to the project at hand. The man who proposed to build the watchtower in his vineyard decided how much he at that time could devote to building it. The parable does not suggest that that was all that the man had. That amount was what the man was willing to commit to the building of the tower. The king was willing to commit ten thousand of his troops to meet the enemy who was approaching. This does not suggest he had only ten thousand troops but he was willing to commit only ten thousand troops to this project. In the light of the work that was to be done the man decided how much he would commit out of what he had to the matter at hand. Now, our Lord was saying to those would-be disciples, when you consider this matter of discipleship, I am not asking if you are willing to commit ten or twenty or thirty or fifty percent to Me, I am demanding that you commit one hundred percent of what you have to Me. If you are not willing to commit everything, if you are not willing to recognize My absolute right over every material thing that I have given to you, you cannot be My disciple.

This requirement was based, first of all, on the recognition that God already owns all things, they are His; and any material thing that we have is a trust from Him. It belongs to Him by right of creation and He has entrusted it to us as a stewardship and we are responsible to administer that stewardship for Him. We are responsible in that administration to Him. This requirement was based further on a recognition of the fact that Jesus Christ by His death has purchased us to Himself and we are His, not only by creation, but also by virtue of redemption, a purchase that makes us doubly His. By virtue of redemption, all that we have is His and He does not renounce His rights to it simply because He has entrusted it to us.

In the light of the Biblical affirmation that all things are His and are only a trust to us, we come back to our original proposition. We are embezzlers from God if we misuse, if we appropriate for ourselves, if we repudiate His right to dispose of and dispense as He wills anything that God has given to us as a trust. We are embezzlers because we have thought that anything that we own, anything that we earn, anything that we purchase is ours. That is what the world says but it is not what the Word says. It is His. This brings an entirely new attitude toward material things on the part of one who is a disciple of Jesus Christ.

The disciple recognizes that everything he has belongs to God. The question he faces then is not how much he must give to God, but how much of what he has that belongs to God will God give him permission to use for himself? If I spend 25¢ for a loaf of bread without God's permission, I have embezzled from God. The fact that I am hungry does not make it right for me to embezzle. The one who owns it must give His permission for me to use it.

It is tragically true that in our giving we are not guided by this concept of discipleship and stewardship. We are guided by income tax laws. We give to gain tax advantage and we assure our tax advantage before we give. Remove the tax advantage and giving stops. The limits set to our giving are not the limits set by the Word of God but the limits of our tax advantage. Is that discipleship? Is that recognition that all that you have belongs to the Lord Jesus Christ and you are His stewards? Ask concerning every penny He puts in your hand: "Lord, how do You direct me to use this?"

God is not stingy. He is not going to withhold from you any good thing. He will permit you to use much of what is His for your own desires, but He wants you to ask His permission before you use it. How much better it is to ask the Lord to let you have that thing you wanted to satisfy you. Get His permission so that you know you haven't cheated Him when you buy it. The question for the disciple is not how much he should give, but how much of what is already God's does he have a right to use for himself?

"Whosoever he be of you that forsaketh not *all* that he hath [whosoever he be of you who does not renounce his rights to *anything* that he has — whosoever he be of you who does not recognize the rights of Jesus Christ to *all* that he has] cannot be my disciple." In the light of the teaching of the Word of God, we stand convicted of embezzlement. Need we continue as embezzlers? When we recognize His rights to all we have and permit Him to dispense that which He has entrusted to us, we are no longer embezzlers, we are good stewards. May God make us good stewards of the grace of God that we may merit His approval in our stewardship so as to be disciples in truth.

9 Prayer and Discipleship

Luke 11:1–10

The intimate relationship which existed between the Lord Jesus Christ and His Father during the days of His earthly life brought a deep conviction to the hearts of the disciples. They frequently saw the Lord Jesus withdraw from His ministry to the multitudes (which consumed much of His time), to be alone with the Father. Our Lord was intimately associated with the Twelve whom He had chosen to be with Him, yet not even that intimate relationship could keep the Son from enjoying an intimate fellowship with the Father.

As the disciples observed this intimacy, they realized that they did not have such an intimacy with the Father as the Lord had. On one occasion when Christ returned from an extended period of praying, they could contain themselves no longer and they blurted out the words recorded in Luke 11:1, "Lord, teach us to pray, as John also taught his disciples." *Lord, teach us to pray.* They recognized that, while they could be believers in the Lord, they could not be true disciples of the Lord until they had learned to pray to the Father as the Lord Jesus prayed — and until they enjoyed an intimacy with the Father such as He enjoyed.

The question the disciples asked seems unnecessary to us, for most of us from early years have been accustomed to hearing men pray. Whether it be father at the dinner table thanking the Lord for food, or a parent leading children in prayer at night, a pastor leading a congregation in prayer in public worship, we are accustomed to the privilege of prayer. It is difficult for us to put ourselves in the environment in which the disciples found themselves. For, while there were those in the Old Testament who from their writings obviously enjoyed communion with God, such was not the widespread experience of the children of Israel. Prayer seems to have had a small part in public worship in the nation Israel. When people went to the Tabernacle, they went to offer sacrifices, to atone for sin by the offering of blood, and there was very little instruction in personal, intimate fellowship which could exist between a believer in the Old Testament and his heavenly Father.

Much of the instruction that came to the disciples came from observing the Pharisees. The Pharisees were extremely ritualistic about their praying but, as you remember from our Lord's words as recorded in the sixth chapter of Matthew, the Pharisees prayed as hypocrites. His words were these, verse 5: "When thou prayest, thou shalt not be as the hypocrites are: for they love to pray standing in the synagogues and in the corners of the streets, that they may be seen of men. Verily I say unto you, They have their reward." Their reward was that they accomplished what they had set out to do. They were seen of men. The prayer of the Pharisee was not addressed to God. It was addressed to the populous passing by that the people might be impressed with the piety of the prayers. The Pharisees prayed not in the Temple where God revealed Himself in the Shekinah glory that was manifested at the Mercy Seat. They went out into the public market place. We would readily conclude that this is a place perhaps the least conducive to praying of any place they could possibly have chosen, but it did accomplish what they set out to do; to impress people with their piety. So, they stood with their hands lifted heavenward, but addressed their prayers to the people who were passing by. Our Lord called them hypocrites because prayer is fellowship between a believer and God. It is not to be a communique between man and men.

To counteract this false example of prayer that was set by the Pharisees, our Lord in Matthew 6:6 said, "When thou prayest, enter into thy closet [a secret place], and when thou hast shut thy door, pray to thy Father which is in secret." He was impressing them that prayer was a matter between the believer and his Father in heaven, not a matter between a believer and men. This did not preclude fellowship of believers in prayer but it did preclude the use of prayer as a hypocritical means of persuading a person of his piety.

The disciples who had been given an example of prayer by the Pharisees had had a second lesson in prayer. The Lord referred to that in Matthew 6:7. It was the lesson that was given by the heathen or by the Gentiles. Our Lord referred to the fact that the Gentiles used vain repetitions: "for they think that they shall be heard for their much speaking." The prayer of the Gentiles, while addressed to the deity and not addressed to the people passing by, was a prayer that was designed to inform the deity of their needs. This prayer assumed that their gods were ignorant, that they had no knowledge of the needs of those who looked to them for help. Their prayer, then, had to be prayed over and over and over again, so that it would finally sink into the consciousness of the Deity that they addressed that they were there, that they had needs, and they were looking for divine help. This completely warped the Biblical concept of God who is sovereign, infinite in His wisdom and knowledge, acquainted with every need of each of His children, and who does not need to be informed as to what those needs are.

Now there had been an ignorance of any real doctrine of prayer on the part of the nation Israel. They had the example of the Pharisees who loved to pray in the market places to commend themselves to God and to contrast themselves with other men. But that did not give them a Biblical doctrine of prayer. The Israelites knew the heathen concept that a god had to be informed because he was basically ignorant. That did not equip them to pray. Watching our Lord's intimate fellowship with the Father day after day after day, they realized their lack of understanding, their lack of indoctrination in what constituted praying. They were convicted that they could not be true disciples unless they understood what it was to pray; therefore they came to petition the Lord, "Lord, teach us to pray."

The word that is used for prayer in the New Testament is a most interesting word. It is the word that literally means *to be like a dog before* someone. At first glance, this seems a rather strange word to use for a child approaching his Father — to be like a dog. But we must remember that the nation among whom our Lord lived was sustained largely by tending flocks and herds. A shepherd would have his dog. Much of the work of tending the sheep was done by the shepherd's dog. The trained dog was at it's master's side and waited on its master for its orders. It did not run ahead of the master, for the dog did not know the direction in which the shepherd desired to move the sheep. The dog waited for instructions. It depended on, submitted to, and obeyed the word of the master. The dog was dependent on the master for its sustenance. He had no right to go into the flock and pick out a young lamb for his own dinner. That concept,

to wait like a dog on its master, was the word that is commonly used
of a believer's approach to God in prayer.

The child of God is dependent on God. He looks to the hand of
his Master for a signal to tell him when to move and when to stay.
He is called back to the Master's side by a word or the sound of a
note on the shepherd's pipe. He attends constantly on the word and
the will of the Master. When the disciples asked the Lord to teach
them to pray, they were not saying simply, "Lord, teach us to say our
prayers." That can be a mechanical thing. They were saying, "Lord,
teach us all that is involved in depending on God as our Master the
same way the faithful dog depends on his master."

A disciple is a servant of his Lord and Master. He is to be in complete and total subjection to the will of his Master. He is to do that
which the Master says to do; and to know that which the Master
teaches; and to love that which the Master approves. When the disciples say, "Lord, teach us to pray," they are saying, "Lord, teach us
all that is involved in depending totally and completely on a master."
God is not only our Father, He is our Lord and our Master; we are
His servants or His disciples.

In Luke 11:2-4 our Lord outlines some of the areas about which a
true disciple, who is a pray-er, will be concerned. The disciples in
their immaturity in the doctrine of prayer possibly used this as their
prayer. Many times children first learning to stammer a prayer to
God use the same form again and again. What a tragedy, when the
child has grown to maturity, to find the child of God still repeating the
same childlike petition in the same form. This prayer was not given
to be the prayer prayed by mature disciples. It was given more to
guide the disciples into the areas about which they should be concerned in their exercise of discipleship in prayer.

May we briefly outline these to you. The first petitions are occupied
with the Father. The prayer begins with a recognition of what God
is in His absolute and unalterable holiness. He is a Father who is
sovereign over all because His dwelling is not here in the earth. He
dwells in the heaven and is sovereign over all. The disciple who prays
as our Lord prayed will be occupied with the person of his Father
primarily, preeminently, before he is occupied with his own need.

Our Lord then progresses from the worship of the Father to the
Father's work in the next petition, "Thy kingdom come. Thy will be
done, as in heaven, so in earth." Those who have traced the presentation our Lord makes of Himself in the gospels are familiar with the
fact that He introduced Himself as a King in fulfillment of all that

God had covenanted to Abraham and David. Christ came as David's son to sit on David's throne, and to rule. He came to subject the nations of the earth to His authority in order that He might reign as King of kings and Lord of lords. The King was also to be a redeemer, and He was to subject a redeemed people to His authority and the authority of the Father. As our Lord offered Himself, His offer was met by opposition. The nation Israel viciously turned on Him and repudiated His right to rule; they rejected the offer of salvation which He made to men through His death on the cross. It seemed as though the purposes of God were thwarted by the evil one and the program of God was nullified by the disobedience of men. Yet our Lord instructed these disciples to petition God that He in His own time and in His own way would fulfill that which He had covenanted with the patriarchs of old. They were to pray that the day would come when Jesus Christ would be enthroned on earth, and that He would reign from sea to sea and from shore to shore, and that a body of redeemed would enjoy the benefits of His reign. It was this kingdom for which they were to pray.

Our Lord said, then, that the disciples were not only to be concerned with the person of the Father but the work of the Father as well. Bringing this down to our day, it certainly means that a disciple cannot be disinterested in that which God is doing through His chosen servants even to the ends of the earth. It means we assume a responsibility not only for the local work in which we are interested, as we certainly will be, but also for God's work through our missionaries to the ends of the earth. God places a responsibility upon us who support the missionaries materially to undergird them spiritually in the warfare in which they are engaged. It involves not only our area of limited knowledge, but it places upon us a responsibility to know what God is doing and where God is working and the channels through which He is working, so that we by prayer can support God's work even to the ends of the earth.

Our very ignorance of what God is doing in different areas and places and through different agencies and channels makes it impossible for us to be the true disciples that Jesus Christ intended us to be; and we are content to be ignorant. Information that ought to move us to prayer rather bores us. Jesus Christ said that the one who is a true disciple of Jesus Christ will be concerned with the work of God even to the ends of the earth.

The third area brings us from God's person and God's work to the needs of the individual himself, "Give us day by day our daily bread."

This registers a total, complete dependence upon God. Man by nature is independent and self-sufficient, and in the economic set-up we have today most anyone can either provide for himself or Uncle Sam will do it for him, so there seems to be little need to petition God for daily bread. The true disciple recognizes that God is the author of every good and perfect gift, and that all we have comes from Him. To petition God concerning these petty, daily needs registers a total, complete dependence upon the Master by the disciple. It is taking the place of a dog dependent on the master for his daily need.

The fourth area to which the Lord directed their attention was the area of forgiveness of sins, the area of cleansing, "forgive us our sins." He was speaking concerning the forgiveness of the child of God from the defilement in his daily walk. This is not a plea for salvation but a plea for restoration to fellowship. When one approaches God whose name is Holy, he instinctively recognizes his own unholiness. Sin, perhaps, keeps more people away from prayer meeting than any other single cause, for we cannot approach the presence of a holy God without being convicted of our unholiness, and that conviction demands a dealing with whatever displeases God. Rather than deal with that in his life which makes him unacceptable in his approach to God, the average individual will withdraw himself from the face of God. A believer recognizes that he has sinned, but a true disciple is willing to deal with that sin.

First John 1:9 reveals the abundant provision God has made so that the sinning saint might have the right to approach the throne of God; but it is the mark of a true disciple that the one who recognizes his sin deals with that sin. Therefore, our Lord instructs His disciples to pray concerning the forgiveness of sins. This is necessary in the natural realm, for two individuals who are in conflict with each other cannot live in harmony. If it is true in the natural realm that there is no harmony, companionship and fellowship apart from unity, so between the child and his Father there can be no fellowship, no harmony, no enjoyment of his unity in the family until that thing which obstructs is dealt with and taken out of the way. This is what the Lord had in mind when He said, "for we also forgive everyone that is indebted to us," that is, we in the natural realm forgive to effect restoration. The mark of a disciple is that he is willing to deal with sin in his life in order that he might enjoy fellowship with the Father.

Then, the final area that the disciples were instructed to pray about was the area of protection or deliverance from the attacks of the evil one, "Lead us not into temptation; but deliver us from evil [or the evil one]." Our Lord recognized that His disciples were dwelling in hostile territory, the enemy's territory. They were surrounded by adversaries on every hand. The child of God, in himself, is incapable of waging war against the hosts arrayed against him. As the Apostle Paul tells us, our warfare is not in the earth nor in the flesh. Our warfare is in the heavenlies. The child of God who deems himself sufficient for the battle will certainly go down in defeat, and a defeated Christian is not a true disciple. When one recognizes his own inability, his own weakness, his own immaturity, and comes in prayer to cast himself on the Father for today's battle, he is a disciple indeed.

Our Lord briefly outlined the different areas in which a disciple would register his complete and total dependence upon God. After He did this, in the parable that our Lord told as it is recorded in Luke 11:5-10, He gave His disciples a lesson on what constitutes the prayer of a true disciple. The illustration that our Lord gave was quite plain. Late at night a man had unexpected guests who came to his home. According to the laws of hospitality of that day, the host was responsible to provide food for them. When he went to the cupboard, he found that all the bread his wife had baked early that morning for the day's needs had been consumed. There would be no baking until the next morning. Consequently, the man had a responsibility which he could not meet. So he went to a friend whom he knew could supply this need, and he petitioned that friend by presenting his need. The friend had already retired for the night. From his bed-chamber he listened to the need but refused to assist the petitioner. The intercessor sensed his responsibility and persisted in prayer. He was determined that he would not go away empty-handed. He repeated his request until it was granted. This man saw himself in the position of a mediator. He was the mediator between a man who had a need and the one who could meet his need. That is what a pray-er is, a mediator between a man in need — whether it be his own or someone else's — and the one who can meet that need. The man persisted in his praying with the result (verse 8), "Though he will not rise and give him, because he is his friend, yet because of his importunity he will rise and give him as many as he needeth." The old English word *importunity* used here meant *persistent asking*. Because of his persistent asking he would rise and give him as much as he needed.

Our Lord is not suggesting that the Father turns a deaf ear to the petitions of His children or to the cry of the intercessor who represents the need of others. That would be a misuse of this parable. Our Lord is teaching that the true disciple persists in waiting upon God on behalf of a need until that need is met. Persistence in prayer characterizes the true praying of a disciple. To drive this lesson home, our Lord said (verse 9) [I render it literally to bring this truth to you]: "Keep on asking and it shall be given you. Keep on seeking and ye shall find. Keep on knocking and it shall be opened unto you. For everyone who keeps on asking, receives; and he who keeps on seeking, finds; and to him who keeps on knocking, it shall be opened."

We certainly would agree that it is necessary to present a petition to God only once, and that God can and will answer that prayer. But the Word says that the disciple who is in as intimate a relationship with the Father as Christ is will be incessant in this matter of praying. Always seeking, always knocking, always asking. How does Christ expect us as disciples to pray? The disciple persists, the disciple is instant in season and out of season, the disciple prays without ceasing, the disciple keeps on asking, keeps on seeking, keeps on knocking. I realize that disciple praying does not have to be carried on in a prayer meeting, but I would hate to think that the only disciples we have are those that are at prayer meeting. One can be saved and not be a man of prayer. But one cannot be a disciple and not be a man of prayer. There is no more important work entrusted to the disciple than the work of praying. In your prayer life, can you pass Christ's test of discipleship?

10 The Disciple a Servant

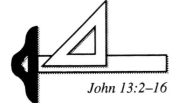

John 13:2–16

Through the years of our Lord's ministry He had been announcing that He was the promised King who was to sit on David's throne and rule over David's house. To the disciples He had revealed Himself as a King on the Mount of Transfiguration when God showed them the glory that would be revealed in the Lord Jesus Christ when He reigns in His Kingdom. The disciples, catching the truth that the Lord Jesus Christ one day would reign as the King of kings and Lord of lords, delighted at the prospect that was theirs of being associated with Him in His reign. Our Lord had promised them that, when He sat on His throne, they would sit on twelve thrones ruling the twelve tribes of Israel. They became obsessed with the position and prominence that would belong to them when our Lord came into His own.

The closer our Lord came to Jerusalem for His last visit, the more the disciples talked about His reign and their position in it. They had completely missed the chronology of events which our Lord revealed to them. He told them that He was going to Jerusalem to die, that His reign on the earth would be postponed for some time, and that at a later time He would return and reign. The disciples blotted out from their minds all His words concerning His death, resurrection, ascension, and absence. They continued to think only of His reign. As they made their way with the Lord to Jerusalem for what was to be His last visit, they were striving with one another all along the way as to who would be greatest. Thinking that our Lord was going to

Jerusalem to mount His throne, they were jockeying for positions of authority in the kingdom. Each one was seeking to put himself in the place of preeminence, second only to the Lord Jesus Christ.

It so happened that the annual Feast of Passover fell as the disciples were in Jerusalem with our Lord. He sent two to prepare the Passover Feast so that He might eat this feast as a memorial of the redemption that God had provided for Israel from Egypt and in anticipation of the redemption that God would provide for Israel and the world. When the disciples came together in the Upper Room, they were thinking not of God's past blessings and deliverance in Egypt, nor were they thinking of that which God would provide in the way of a perfect salvation through the sacrifice of God's own chosen Passover Lamb. They were thinking only of themselves and the position which they would have when Christ ruled and reigned. As they came through the door of that Passover room, they probably went through the ritual of washing the hands and perchance also the feet in the water that was provided for ritualistic cleansing. This was customary, for no Jew could sit down to enjoy a common meal, let alone the Passover Feast, without washing his hands and his feet.

As they went through the ritual of the Passover meal, they watched as the Lord Jesus, the Master of the Feast, early in the Feast, rose from His position at the head of the table and took a basin of water and a towel. It was the custom for the Master of the Feast to go to each guest at the table to present a basin of water in which the guest dipped his fingers and then wiped them on the towel. This was an established part of the ritual by which those at the feast confessed their uncleanness and their need for cleansing. The next part of the meal was for the Master of the Feast to pass around the Passover Lamb. While they partook of the Passover Lamb, they were anticipating the answer to their confessed need as they had expressed it in the ritual of applying water to their hands. Just as the water signified the need for cleansing, the lamb signified God's answer for their need. Their need was to be met through the Lamb of God that taketh away the sin of the world.

As the Lord proceeded through the Passover, the one who found himself at His right hand must have been commending himself; for, thought he, this is the position that I will have when our Lord comes into His kingdom. I have been chosen first among the Twelve. I am in the position of honor. The one at the left hand must have looked with envy on the one at the right and said, "I wonder why he was given the place of preeminence and I was put in the second place;

but, at least, I am chosen above the other ten." To instruct them and
to show them that they were not disciples in truth, our Lord injected
something into this Passover Feast that had never been observed in
a Passover Feast throughout the hundreds of years of its observance.

The Master of the Feast, after the meal was ended, instead of pro-
nouncing a benediction that completed the observance, stood at the
head of the table. He laid aside His robe and took a towel, and He
wrapped the towel around Him. This would have been itself of great
significance to the Twelve. We cannot speak dogmatically, but we do
know that each different strata of society in Israel identified itself by
a different color of ribbon or border on the robe that the men wore.
The fact that Christ was addressed as a rabbi whenever He went into
a strange synagogue suggests that He may have worn a robe bordered
with the ribbon that marked Him as a rabbi. This was one of the most
honored and distinguished callings that a man could have in Israel,
to be an official teacher and interpreter of the law. The towel was the
sign of a servant. It was the badge of his profession, the sign of identification in the lowest office into which one could put himself. According to John 13, after our Lord had completed the Passover meal
and He arose, although without doubt the disciples thought He was
arising to pronounce the benediction, He laid aside that garment of
dignity and honor which He usually wore, and He girded Himself with
a towel.

Our Lord was there as a servant, not a Master. He was there as
one to serve, not one to teach. Jesus was there to perform menial
tasks, not to be waited on. If this had surprised the disciples, without
doubt that which He proceeded to do surprised them even more.
For our Lord took the basin that He had passed earlier in the feast
for ceremonial cleansing, and He proceeded from disciple to disciple
to do the most menial task that a servant could be called on to do,
to wash away the defilement that had been incurred as one was coming to the supper. This idea was so revolting to Peter that, when Christ
began to wash Peter's feet, he said: "Lord, dost thou wash my feet?"
(John 13:6). The emphasis is on the pronoun, "thou." "Does such
an one as You are wash the feet of such a one as I?" This was the one
who earlier had confessed that Jesus was the Messiah, the Son of the
living God. He had recognized that He had come from God, that He
was God come in the flesh, that He was engaged in the work of God,
and had revealed the Father to men. He recognized that this was the
One who was to be crowned with honor and glory, and was destined
to rule as King of kings and Lord of lords. Peter's concept was that

the majesty, the dignity, the honor, the glory that belonged to Jesus Christ precluded Him from doing a servant's work. It was beneath His dignity, beneath His position. He was to be ministered to but He was not to minister.

Our Lord, after He had engaged in the act, gave an interpretation of the significance of the act. He noted in verse 7 that Peter's question arose out of ignorance for He said, "What I do thou knowest not now." Peter understood much about the person and work of Christ, but there was so much that he did not understand. He did not understand that men could be saved and redeemed and cleansed only as the Son of God became a servant of God. As the servant of Jehovah, He gave Himself in obedience to God so that He might become the Saviour of men.

When Peter affirmed, "Thou shalt never wash my feet!" the Lord said to Peter, "If I wash thee not, thou hast no part with me." Peter's heart hungered to be identified with Christ, to be joined with Him in His redemption and in His reign. He wanted to share His Kingdom and His glory. So in effect he pleaded, "Lord, don't stop with my feet, start with my head and go all the way down — give me a full and complete bath."

In verse ten the Lord instructed Peter concerning the benefits that would come to men because He put Himself in a servant's place. His instruction was in these words, "He that is washed [literally bathed all over] needeth not save to wash [sponge] his feet." There are two different words in the original text which emphasized two different results of the Lord Jesus Christ becoming a servant of God that He might serve the needs of men. Two aspects of cleansing are anticipated here. The first aspect is in the first word, washed. In Titus 3:5 we read: "Not by works of righteousness which we have done, but according to his mercy he saved us, by the washing of regeneration [or the washing of the new birth] and renewing of the Holy Ghost; Which he shed on us abundantly through Jesus Christ our Saviour." Our Lord was speaking here of the benefits of His death by which one who comes to trust Jesus Christ as a personal Saviour is cleansed from all sin and all unrighteousness. He is made clean to a degree acceptable to God. He is made as righteous as Jesus Christ is righteous, and he consequently is acceptable to the Father. This is the washing that Christ said would be provided when He, as a servant, was obedient to death that He might meet the needs of men.

The second aspect of cleansing in John 13:10 lies in the words, "he needeth not save to wash his feet." This second washing is the cleansing referred to in I John 1:9, the cleansing of the believer from the defilement of his sins so that he might be restored to fellowship. "If we confess our sins, he is faithful and just to forgive us our sins, and to cleanse us from all unrighteousness." Christ is promising not only the full bath of regeneration because He would be obedient as a servant; He is also promising cleansing for those whose feet are defiled while they are on their pilgrim journey. The truth that He wanted to bring home to Peter was that Peter's need could not be met unless He became a servant, and as a servant He ministered in obedience to God so that, in turn, He might minister to the needs of men.

Had Jesus Christ by-passed the servant's place and all that it entailed in obedience to God, and gone to the throne, there would have been no cleansing. The servant-work was essential if the needs of sinners were to be met.

Now, after our Lord had instructed and interpreted the doctrine involved, He came to make a personal application. In verse twelve He asked the question, "Know ye what I have done to you?" There is no response to this question for the disciples now are silenced by what He has done. They stand convicted of their covetousness, their selfishness, their desire to put themselves in the place of preeminence. The lesson that the Lord of Glory must put Himself in a servant's place seemed to have come through to them and they made no attempt to reply to His question, "Know ye what I have done to you?" Lest they miss the point, our Lord explains it, "Ye call me Master and Lord: and ye say well; for so I am. If I then, your Lord and Master, have washed your feet [if I your Lord and Master have put myself in a servant's place]; ye ought also to wash one another's feet [that is, to put yourselves in a servant's place]. I have given you an example [and the example was not in applying water to feet — the example was in putting oneself into the place of a servant so as to minister to the needs of the others] that ye should do as I have done unto you . . . The servant is not greater than his Lord; neither is he that is sent greater than he that sent him. If ye know these things, happy are ye if ye do them." We find that this whole incident arose primarily because the disciples did not understand what constituted discipleship. Their concept of discipleship was that it elevated them to a position of preeminence. They needed to learn the lesson that discipleship elevated them to the privilege of service and ministry.

They coveted the honor and glory that would be theirs in being associated with Christ — and Christ coveted for them the honor and glory that comes from ministering to others in His name.

To be a disciple is to be a servant, not only a servant of Jesus Christ but also a servant of believers in Jesus Christ, yea, a servant of all those whom God loves and for whom Christ died, in the name of the Lord Jesus Christ. That this lesson was brought home to Peter is quite evident when Peter writes his first epistle — chapter five. There, writing to the elders in verse two, he says, "Feed the flock of God which is among you, taking the oversight." The elders were not viewed in a position of authority. They were viewed as being in a position of responsibility, but the responsibility entailed service on behalf of the sheep. The elders were viewed as being responsible for the oversight of the flock. As such (verse three), they were not to be lords over God's heritage, they were not to put themselves in a position of prominence, they were to be examples to the flock. They were to be servants of the flock. The elders were made responsible as shepherds but their responsibility of necessity involved ministry and service to those for whom they were responsible. Peter, when he writes in verse five, says: "All of you be subject one to another, and be clothed with humility." The interesting thing is that the word translated "clothed" in verse five is exactly the same word as is found in John 13:5 where Christ wiped their feet with the towel with which He was girded or "clothed." It is obvious that Peter's mind as he writes to these elders is going back to John 13 and he is sharing with them the lesson he had learned, that to be a disciple involves service to those in need.

In John 13:3 we find that Christ was willing to put Himself in a servant's position because He knew who He was, He knew where He had come from, and He knew where He was going. He was absolutely secure in His position. John notes that before our Lord laid aside His garment and took the towel, "Jesus knowing that the Father had given all things into his hands, and that he was come from God, and went to God; He riseth from supper, and laid aside his garments; and took a towel, and girded himself." Jesus Christ did not consider putting Himself in a servant's position an act that degraded or made Him inferior. He was not afraid of loss of face, of loss of dignity by putting Himself in the position that no one else wanted. Because He was secure in His Father, He put Himself in the servant's place. It was the insecurity of the disciples in their position that made them jockey for a position and try to gain a place that was not rightfully theirs to attain.

Many, out of a desire to gain prominence and preeminence, and to glorify themselves, refuse to put themselves in a position where it will look as though they are making themselves inferior to someone else. Not until we realize that Jesus Christ, because of His security in His position before the Father, put Himself into the servant's place, will we see our position does not depend on our grasping, our attaining, our coveting, but depends on our doing what Jesus Christ did — putting ourselves in the servant's position that God in due season might exalt us.

It seems to be the concept of our Lord that love and service are interchangeable. One loves a believer when he serves or ministers to the believer. Service to a believer is love for the believer put into action. When our Lord said, "By this shall all men know that ye are my disciples, if ye have love one to another," He was saying, "By this shall all men know that ye are my disciples, if ye serve one another." Why? Because Jesus Christ could not make a man His disciple who was not a servant. Let me ask you this. How long has it been since you have gone to a fellow believer in Christ and said to him, "What can I do to help you?" How long since you have approached the Sunday school superintendent or pastor asking, "How can I help? What can I do?" Our excuse might be, I'm not a teacher. The real reason might be, I'm not a disciple!

Will you hear again the word of our Lord? "If such a one as I, your Lord and Master, have put Myself into the servant's place and demonstrated it by washing feet, you also ought to put yourselves in a servant's place and serve in My name." One may be saved and not a servant, but he may not be a disciple if he is not a servant.

11 The Ministry of Disciples

Mark 6:30–44

In order that many in Israel might be reached with the good news that God had fulfilled His promise and had sent the Redeemer and the Sovereign to that nation, our Lord commissioned the twelve disciples to go and announce throughout the land that the Messiah had come. According to the sixth chapter of the gospel of Mark, when our Lord sent out the Twelve, He gave them a message to preach: "Repent, for the kingdom of heaven is at hand." That their message might be authenticated, the Lord gave the disciples the power to perform the same miracles that He had been performing to authenticate His Person and His Word. The disciples had gone through the length and the breadth of the land to fulfill their ministry. At the expiration of their appointed ministry, they came back to report to the Lord on the success.they had enjoyed. Those men, as they came together, having been separated from the close fellowship with one another that they had enjoyed, must have been bubbling over as they shared with one another the experiences they had had in the ministry. They shared with the Lord Himself that which had been done through the power that had been given to them.

It seems as though our Lord detected that these disciples were developing an entirely erroneous concept of the ministry, and they needed instruction as to what constituted making disciples. The emphasis was not to be upon the miracles they had performed — these were secondary to the word they were to proclaim. Yet, we can understand how, as natural men, they became preoccupied with the manifestations of divine power that had been worked through them. After this special ministry was over, our Lord took the Twelve apart into a mountain so that He might instruct them concerning the nature of the ministry which was to be entrusted to them as His representatives after His departure. John tells us that the period of the Passover was approaching. Because the Passover was designed to provide great spiritual lessons for Israel, lessons that looked back to a past deliverance and forward to a coming Deliverer, so that the disciples might profit by the Passover Feast which they soon would enjoy, our Lord took them aside for a time of rest and refreshment. He took them aside for a time of instruction that He might interpret to them the ministry which had been entrusted to Him and which He, in turn, was entrusting to them. But our Lord could not be hidden. No mountain recess could keep those hungry people of Galilee from searching Him out that they might be taught by Him. Our Lord's time alone with the disciples was all too brief. He was pressed upon by great multitudes who came to hear the words He spoke.

In the incident that we familiarly refer to as the feeding of the five thousand, think of the great lesson which the Lord taught the disciples about the nature of the ministry of a disciple. This was the real purpose of the miracle.

Through the day our Lord had been teaching. It is recorded in Mark 6:34 that, when Jesus saw much people He was moved with compassion toward them because they were as sheep not having a shepherd. He began to teach them many things. Our Lord's ministry was a ministry of teaching. While He performed innumerable miracles, and John testifies to the fact that they were innumerable, He had not come primarily to be a miracle worker. He had not come to amaze people by demonstrations of His divine power and authority. Our Lord had come to impart truth through what He taught concerning the Father. To satisfy the needy, the Lord spent the day teaching. This was the first lesson that Christ wanted to get across to the disciples. Even though for a season He had invested them with the power to work miracles, it was not the miracle worker who was doing the work of a disciple. Our Lord's ministry was a ministry of teaching, a ministry of revealing the Father to men; and He had called them as disciples that they might continue the ministry He had come to carry out. He had come to teach, and as disciples they were to teach to meet the needs of men.

Often it is necessary for men to learn spiritual truth by being given a lesson in the physical or the material world. It is our earnest conviction that the feeding of the five thousand was not primarily for the benefit of the hungry multitudes. The feeding of the five thousand was designed primarily for the benefit of the Twelve. The event was not designed to fill the stomachs of the hungry men. It was designed to enlighten the minds of the ignorant disciples. In order that the disciples might learn a lesson concerning the ministry and service of disciples (which is a truth in the spiritual realm), our Lord set the stage and performed a miracle in the physical realm so that by transference they might learn a great spiritual truth, the truth of what constitutes the ministry of a disciple.

The day had been spent in teaching and hearing the Word of God taught. The populace who came to be taught by our Lord were so satisfied by the spiritual food that was provided for them that they seem to have been totally unconscious of any physical hunger. It was not the multitude who came to the disciples and said, "We are hungry, will you feed us?" As far as the record is concerned, they registered no consciousness of physical hunger themselves. Why? They were so preoccupied with what came from the lips of our Lord as He revealed divine truth concerning the Father to them, that they were unconscious of their physical needs. In this, they were likened to our Lord who spent time ministering to the woman at the well in Sychar. The disciples were concerned with our Lord's physical needs and went to the village to buy food. But, when they came and offered food to the Lord, He said that He had meat to eat that they knew not of, for His meat was to do the will of God. He was sustained by His obedience to the will and the Word of God so that He was not conscious of physical hunger. It was the disciples who were preoccupied with the material, not those who were being taught. They sensed only embarrassment. Here was a multitude for whom no provision had been made, and from the natural standpoint no provision could be made, for they were in a wilderness place. There was no possibility of obtaining food for such a vast crowd.

This set the stage for the lesson that the Lord wanted to teach. He turned to Philip and said, as it is recorded in John's account of this incident, "Philip, whence shall we buy bread, that these may eat?" Philip was the natural one to ask this question for they were in Philip's home territory. If you, while traveling, want to find a good restaurant, you find a native of the area and ask him where there is a good place to eat. Philip would know the available sources of supply. Philip confessed the utter impossibility of finding any natural means of supplying the physical hunger of this multitude.

The disciples were up against a blank wall. They had no means whatsoever of meeting the needs of this people. The disciples' solution for the problem they faced was to send the people away. That, in effect, said they had no responsibility in the problem — it was up to the people. If they didn't have foresight enough to bring food along for the day, what happened was no responsibility of the disciples. Send them away and let them fend for themselves. But our Lord recognized an obligation and He said to the disciples, "Give ye them to eat" (Mark 6:37). The disciples were overwhelmed at the responsibility that the Lord had placed upon them. They were fully cognizant of their inability to meet the need. That is exactly the position in which the Lord wanted them. He wanted them to confess their utter helplessness to do that which He commanded them to do.

The Lord is not putting upon the disciples the responsibility of feeding the poor of the world. Many men are asking the question today, "What is the role of the church in relation to the problem of poverty in our nation and across the face of the earth?" This passage is used by those who believe that it is the responsibility of the church to feed the physically hungry. Notice, please, in this passage that our Lord was primarily concerned not with the physical hunger but with the spiritual hunger. Had He been concerned with the physical hunger, He would have told the disciples to bake bread so that the multitude could be fed. No, our Lord was concerned with their spiritual needs. And He was not entrusting to the disciples the responsibility of taking care of the hungry multitudes. He was using their physical hunger to bring home to them a truth that as disciples they were to minister to the spiritual needs of the multitudes as He had spent the whole day doing. This was the obligation that rested upon a disciple: "Give ye them to eat."

Our Lord was viewing the disciples in this incident as shepherds. He was viewing the multitude before Him as sheep. It was not the responsibility of sheep to seek out the shepherd to be fed. It was the responsibility of the shepherd to lead the sheep to water and to food. Our Lord commented in verse 34 that He "was moved with compassion toward them, because they were as sheep not having a shepherd." There were many in Israel who called themselves shepherds. The Pharisees called themselves shepherds in Israel, and they had assumed the responsibility of feeding the sheep, but the flock was starving to death for there was no nourishment in what the Pharisees put before the people as spiritual food. There was nothing in Pharisaism that could satisfy a hungry soul. To tell a man to keep the Law perfectly, and promise that if he kept the Law perfectly he would be accepted of God was no food, because no man could keep the Law. The Sadducees with their ritualism in the Levitical system insisted on the observance of all the feasts and holy days of Israel, but there was no food in that which Sadducees put before the people for they tasted that which the Sadducees presented and found that it was dry in their mouths. There were multitudes who called themselves shepherds but none to do the work of a shepherd. Now, against that background of a starving people, the Lord said to the Twelve, "You do the work of a shepherd. If you are My disciples, you will feed the sheep." Or to put it another way, "I came to give men the bread of life and the water of life, and, if you are My disciples, you will do what I have been doing. You will carry on and continue the work that I have done throughout My earthly ministry. . . . Give ye them to eat."

Of himself a man has nothing that he can give another that will meet his spiritual need, slake his thirst and satisfy his spiritual hunger. And the disciples — mark it well — could perform a multiplicity of miracles and still not feed sheep. For that which created amazement and wonder and awe would leave a man as spiritually empty as before he beheld the miracle. This is the lesson that our Lord is trying to get across to them in their present preoccupation with the miracles that they had been performing. It was not Christ's miracles that fed men, it was the Word of God that He taught them that satisfied their spiritual hunger.

The record is familiar to you. The disciples mingled with the crowd and came back to report that the only food that could be found among the multitude could be held in one hand — five little biscuits and two small fish. Can you imagine the embarrassment of the disciples when, after they went through the crowd and returned, this was the best they could present to Him? It was a confession of their inability to fulfill that which Christ had told them to do, to feed sheep. This seems to reflect on our Lord, for He seems to be making an unreasonable request. It almost seems that they were thinking, "Lord, don't You want to change that order You gave us in the light of these circumstances? Isn't there something else You would rather we do?" But our Lord took that which they presented, inadequate, insufficient as it was, and multiplied that which had been placed in His hands, while it was in His hands, so that from Him the disciples received that which they in turn could give to the crowd. The secret here was not how much they had nor what they had but the One whom they had. He was able to take that which from the human standpoint they were utterly inadequate to do, that which He commanded them to do, and was able to do it. As the disciples distributed to the crowd that which was multiplied in the hand of Christ, the multitude was satisfied.

What is Christ trying to teach the disciples about the nature of their ministry? It can be summarized simply this way: Jesus Christ called them and then commissioned them as disciples to do for men what He had come to do for men. He was commissioning them to continue the work in which He had been engaged. The feeding of the 5,000 was the illustration. In the gospel of John, we find the word of our Lord that specifically entrusted this ministry to them. Notice John 15:26, 27: "When the Comforter is come, whom I will send unto you from the Father, even the Spirit of truth, which proceedeth from the Father, he shall testify of me: And ye also shall bear witness." Please consider several things in these verses. The Spirit who is called here the Spirit of truth, that is, the Spirit who communicates truth, will testify of Christ: And ye, also, in addition to the Spirit, will testify of Me. We see a parallelism here: the disciples are being entrusted with the ministry of telling men about Jesus Christ — ye shall testify of Me. But they are not to do it alone. They can not do it alone any more than they could feed the 5,000 alone. They needed divine assistance to testify of Christ. What divine assistance is provided? Verse 26: "The Spirit of truth, which proceedeth from the Father, he shall testify of me." It was the Son of God plus the disciples who ministered to the physical needs of men in the feeding of the 5,000. It is the disciples plus the Spirit of God who will meet the spiritual needs of men when they do the ministry of a disciple.

In John 17 we have a further explanation concerning this ministry of disciples. John 17:4 reads: "I have finished the work which thou gavest me to do." You will notice immediately that this word was spoken before Christ had gone to the cross. The finished work, then, could not refer to the cross work of Christ, for that was as yet unfinished. What work, then, was He referring to when He said, "I have finished the work which thou gavest me to do"? In John 1:18 we are told that Christ came that He might reveal the Father to men. Christ came as a revealer. He came as an introducer. Our Lord came to teach men truths concerning the Father that men might know the Father. One of the principal works in which Christ was engaged was the work of revealing the Father. That is why you have so much emphasis throughout the gospels on Christ's teaching. He was teaching to reveal the Father to men. Now that Christ has come to the end of His earthly ministry, He can say, "I have finished that work of revealing the Father that You gave Me to do." That this is what our Lord had in mind is quite clear from verse six, where, referring to the finished work, He says, "I have manifested [or revealed] thy name unto the men which thou gavest me." "I have made the Father known — I have finished the work. I have done My work as a teacher." Then in verse 8 He says, "I have given unto them the words. . . ." and again in verse 14, "I have given them thy word. . . ." This refers to the work of the teacher who has imparted truth to those who are His disciples. But this committing the word to the disciples is more than simply teaching them. What Christ is saying is, "I have taught them and now I have given them a commission as to what they should do with that which I taught."

In John 17:18 there is this commission: "As thou hast sent me into the world, even so have I also sent them into the world." Read the verse this way: For the same purpose for which You sent Me into the world, even so have I also sent them into the world. Do you get the connection? The Son says to the Father in this great prayer, "You sent Me into the world to reveal the Father to men, and I have finished that work of revealing the Father to men. I have given the word that You gave Me to these disciples, and now I send them out into the world to do exactly what You sent Me into the world to do — to reveal the Father by teaching men the truth of the Word of God." The disciple was a recipient of revelation and then he was commissioned to disseminate that revelation that had been given to him. He was to be a light in the midst of darkness; he was to provide spiritual food for those who were hungry; he was to make available life for those who were dead in sin. He had no ability, no power of himself to do it, but the Spirit of God had been given to him to energize him so that he and the Spirit should reveal the Father and the way to the Father to men. By the feeding of the 5,000 in chapter six of Mark these men were taught the lesson that they were to receive from Christ that which they could distribute to meet the needs of men. Now they received a specific commission as the Son in John 17 says, "I have completed the work of revealing the Father; I have deposited this truth with men and now I send them into the world for the same purpose that You sent Me into the world."

When we come to the close of our Lord's earthly sojourn, we find our Lord giving a commission. Although this is familiar to you, look at it again in Matthew 28:18 — "All power [or authority] is given unto me in heaven and earth." Since He has all authority, Christ has the right to appoint His representatives and to commission them in the work which they are to do. The one who has the authority makes an appointment, and this is His appointment: "Go ye therefore, and [literally] make disciples of all nations." What is the sign that men have become disciples? They are baptized. How do you make them disciples? By teaching them. There were to make disciples by teaching them. Teaching them what? Whatsoever I have commanded you. This is built upon John 17. I have revealed the Father to them — they have received a knowledge of the Father from Me; therefore, I send them out into the world to continue doing what I have been doing during the years of My earthly sojourn. Then on the eve of the ascension, our Lord said, "You go and you make disciples of all nations by teaching them what I, taught you."

As we put these passages of Scripture together, we come to the unshakeable conclusion that the ministry of a disciple is the ministry of introducing Jesus Christ to men who do not know Him. The ministry of a disciple is the ministry of imparting to others the truth concerning the Father and the Son that has been revealed to us by the Holy Spirit. The ministry of a disciple makes one a channel through which the Spirit of God brings divine truth home to men who are ignorant of God because of their natural blindness.

Men are not disciples because of what they give or what they do.

They are disciples because of what they communicate to others about Jesus Christ. We recognize that Christ had two principal ways by which He communicated truth about the Father to the disciples. These are referred to many times but John 14 summarizes them. If anyone has any question about the Person of Christ, there are two witnesses as to His Person: His works and His words. His words came from the Father and were a revelation of the Father to men. His works were performed by the Father and were a testimony to His words. It leads to the conclusion that we carry out the ministry of a disciple in two principal ways, by our lives and by our lips. One without the other is unsufficient and inadequate. The Word of God that comes from the lips of the disciple must be corroborated by the works of God in the life of the disciple. When life and lip are in harmony so that the Word of God is being presented and the truth concerning Christ is being lived and taught, one is doing the service of a disciple.

We were placed as salt in the earth. Salt creates a thirst. The life of a disciple can create an insatiable thirst in another individual for Jesus Christ — but the life itself does not give a man anything to believe to become a child of God and a disciple. The life must be supported by the word, and the word and the life will bring a man to a knowledge of Jesus Christ.

What does God demand of you as His disciple? Feed hungry men. Give ye them to eat. Until men are hearing about Jesus Christ, and seeing His life from your life and your lips, you are not fulfilling the obligation which was placed on you as a disciple. The commission is not fulfilled by your contribution to a missionary budget that sends a missionary to some dark place of the earth. The Great Commission is fulfilled when you, right where you are, disciple somebody else by teaching them and showing them what you have learned of the things of Christ and the Father from the Word of God. May God make us disciples who feed sheep where we live day by day.

12 The Fellowship of Disciples

Mark 3:6–14

The Lord Jesus Christ from all eternity past had enjoyed a personal intimate fellowship with the Father, for the Father and the Son were One. When the Lord Jesus Christ left the presence of the Father and came into this world, He continued His fellowship with the Father. As we read through the gospels, we find that the Lord Jesus Christ lived His earthly life in personal intimate fellowship with the Father. This desire for fellowship with the Father frequently took Him away from His companionship with men to spend a night on the hillside alone with the Father. But when the Lord Jesus Christ came in the flesh, He not only desired and did continue His fellowship with the Father, He desired fellowship with men as well. Men by nature are gregarious creatures. They do not enjoy being alone; they were not created to exist alone. Men were created to live in fellowship with others with whom they could enjoy fellowship. Since the Lord Jesus Christ possessed a full, complete and true humanity, He desired fellowship with men during the time of His incarnation. When our Lord chose twelve men whom He was to call His apostles, we read in Mark 3:14 that He had two purposes in mind for them. "He ordained twelve, that they should be with him, and that he might send them forth to preach." The first purpose was fellowship, the second purpose was service. "He ordained twelve, that they should be with him" — fellowship; "and that he might send them forth to preach" — service.

In previous studies on the subject of discipleship, we have discovered that a disciple is a servant. He is to set aside his own will in order that he might do the will of the Master who has called him to be His servant. It would be so easy for us to become involved in our service for Jesus Christ we would forget that in our Lord's statement of the purpose for which He called the disciples the preeminent thing was not service but personal intimate fellowship with Himself.

Our Lord longed for fellowship with those whom He had chosen and whom He would appoint to some ministry in His name, and unless we satisfy His heart in the fellowship which we enjoy with Him, we are not discharging our stewardship nor are we true disciples. Fellowship is the response of total personality to another person. The Lord Jesus Christ had a body of truth to present to men. He was God come in the flesh to reveal God to men who were in the flesh. This body of truth was entrusted to Him by the Father to communicate to men. So our Lord had a ministry to the minds of men. He had come to enlighten minds that were darkened by sin. He had come to teach minds that were devoid of any truth or knowledge concerning God because they could not by natural reasoning find out God. The Lord Jesus Christ spent a great deal of His time teaching. He taught the multitudes the elemental truths concerning God, the way of access to God, the demands which God made upon those who would walk in fellowship with Him, and presented God's way of salvation from sin to men who were lost. But to those who became His disciples, our Lord taught deeper truths concerning that which God had committed to Him to reveal. In Mark 4:34, after He had told a number of parables in order to communicate truth to men who were in darkness, He said: "Without a parable spake he not unto them: and when they were alone, he expounded all things to his disciples." He taught them! In John 8 our Lord spoke at some length of His ministry of teaching. Beginning in John 8:28 we read, "Then said Jesus unto them, When ye have lifted up the Son of man, then shall ye know that I am he, and that I do nothing of myself; but as my Father hath taught me, I speak these things. And he that sent me is with me: the Father hath not left me alone; for I do always those things that please him. As he spake these words, many believed on him. Then said Jesus to those Jews which believed on him, If ye continue in my word, then are ye my disciples indeed; And ye shall know the truth, and the truth shall make you free." Discipleship was not possible unless one *knew* the word which Christ had taught, *believed* the word, then *remained* in that word and made that word his light. If one is to have fellowship with the Master, the disciple must be taught. Our Lord in bringing men into fellowship with Himself desired that men should enter into the truth that He had come to communicate to them.

Jesus Christ not only ministered to the minds of men but He ministered to their hearts as well, for this is a great area of human experience and the heart is an essential part of personality. The Lord Jesus Christ came to minister to the hearts of men. Think of John's testimony, for instance, in John 13:1: "Now before the feast of the passover, when Jesus knew that his hour was come that he should depart out of this world unto the Father, having loved his own which were in the world, he loved them unto the end." He loved them! This was the heart of the Lord Jesus going out to minister to the hearts of those whom He had called to be His disciples. It was more than affection. This was a tender care and concern for the welfare of those who were the objects of His affection. In physical weakness, He was their strength. In times of persecution, He was their protection. In times of want, He was their provision. Every area of need He supplied. And this supply was the demonstration and expression of His love for them. His disciples were not only enlightened in the mind, they were provided for by His love.

The Lord came, in addition, to minister to the area of the will. For an enlightened mind and a stirred heart do not in themselves make one a disciple. Not until the will responds to what a man has been given to know and to the person who has loved him does one become a disciple in fellowship with his master. Our Lord had come to do the will of the Father and He did the will of the Father perfectly. Now, He has come to put His will before the disciples in order that they might respond to His will. That was involved in our Lord's statement in Luke 9:23, "If any man will come after me, let him deny [say no to] himself, and take up his cross daily, and follow me." Our Lord said that one could not be a disciple until he said no to his goals and plans and ambitions for his own life and accepted Christ's plan for his life. This was to be a daily experience for the disciple, the experience of walking in complete dependence upon the strength of God and obedience to the will of God.

Now when the mind is in harmony with the mind of the Master, and the heart responds to the love of the Master, and the will obeys the will of the Master, one is in fellowship with the Master. Our Lord had come to choose these men and set them apart to this peculiar experience, the experience of knowing Him and of loving Him and of obeying Him. "He ordained twelve, that they might be with him."

From all eternity past our Lord had sovereign authority. Angels knew Him because they ministered in His presence. When He spoke to angels, they leaped to obey. They were ministering spirits, obedient to the Sovereign they recognized, but they were not disciples. They knew God and they obeyed God but no angel was called a disciple. To know is not enough. One becomes a disciple when he enters into a deep, personal, intimate fellowship with the one whom he knows because he loves that one and gives himself in complete obedience to that one.

In Luke's gospel there is an illustration of this fellowship that makes one a disciple. Luke 10:38-42 gives the familiar incident concerning Martha and Mary in their relationship to Jesus Christ: "Now it came to pass, as they went, that they entered into a certain village: and a certain woman named Martha received him into her house. And she had a sister called Mary, which also sat at Jesus' feet, and heard his word. But Martha was cumbered about much serving, and came to him, and said, Lord, dost thou not care that my sister hast left me to serve alone? bid her therefore that she help me. And Jesus answered and said unto her, Martha, Martha, thou art careful and troubled about many things: But one thing is needful: and Mary has chosen that good part, which shall not be taken away from her."

If you had asked Martha, "Martha, are you a disciple?" I am certain you would have received a ready affirmative answer. Martha was a disciple of Jesus Christ. She proved her discipleship by her service for the Lord Jesus Christ. Our Lord came into the little village of Bethany and received hospitality in her home. According to verse 38 it was Martha who had extended Him this hospitality — not Lazarus or Mary. It was Martha who invited Him into her home. If you had asked Martha, "Why did you extend hospitality to the Lord Jesus?" she would have said, "It was because I am His disciple." That was not the end of her demonstration of discipleship. She went beyond that, for Martha went to a great deal of trouble to provide for our Lord's physical needs.

"Martha was cumbered about much serving." Martha was not content to prepare a quick dinner, not content to warm up some of yesterday's leftovers. It would have been easy to set that before the Lord and satisfy needs. But Martha through her service was trying to show the extent of her discipleship and she desired to take care of His physical needs in the best manner possible. "Martha, are you a disciple?" "Haven't I proved it by entertaining Him and providing the finest dinner possible for Him?" But as we read this we cannot escape the fact that there is something lacking in Martha's discipleship. You could not ask her to work any harder nor to do more nor to sacrifice more for the Lord's sake, but her sacrifice and her service do not of themselves make her a full and true disciple. That is why our attention is focused on Mary.

It is said in verse 39 that "She had a sister called Mary, which also sat at Jesus' feet, and heard his word." Notice a little word in this statement that we would be tempted to pass over that gives us a clue as to what our Lord is trying to convey — the little word "also." That means that in addition to what Martha did, Mary did something else. This does not suggest that Mary was not busy in preparing for our Lord's physical needs. But, in addition to what Martha did, in which Mary had a part, she added that ingredient that constituted her an approved disciple. She sat at Jesus' feet and heard His word. Martha was occupied for Christ. Mary was occupied with Christ. That made the difference. Involvement in service without being involved with the Person who has commissioned us as His servants does not satisfy the heart of the Lord Jesus. Thus His commendation was on Mary. He had to say, "Martha, Martha, thou art careful to be a good hostess and provide for My bodily needs, and you gave attention to all the details but one thing is needful." The needful thing was not to put food on the table. The needful thing was to give attention to a person.

Martha was doing for Him. Mary was receiving from Him. Our Lord did not come to be ministered unto but to minister. He did not come to be waited on, He came to seek those who let Him minister to them. When Mary sat to hear words that enlightened her mind, that moved her heart, and brought her to obedience to Him, our Lord was satisfied for He had found a true disciple.

Service often has that which can be measured in it. We can see a person busy doing something for the Lord. The very time we spend, the energy that we expend gives us a sense of satisfaction and approval. Fellowship is not something you can see. We tend to evaluate men's relationship to Jesus Christ by what they do rather than by what they experience in fellowship with the Lord. We tend to evaluate our own lives in terms of what we are occupied doing for Him instead of evaluating ourselves by the amount of time we spend with Him.

Because our hours are so regimented from dawn till dark, demands are made upon us whether it be at home or at school or in the office. It is so difficult to set aside time to do what Mary did, to enjoy personal, intimate fellowship with the Lord Jesus Christ. But until we learn to do that we cannot be His disciples. No amount of activity on Martha's part was a substitute for that which Mary was giving to the

Lord Jesus Christ. Martha gave her time, her efforts, her strength. Mary gave herself. Our Lord said, "One thing is needful. Mary hath chosen that good part which shall not be taken away from her." One thing is needful if you will fulfill that for which I have chosen you to be My disciple. We were not chosen first to serve, but rather to be with Him. It is more important to be occupied *with* Christ than it is to be occupied *for* Christ.

To the disciples on the Mount of Transfiguration was given one of the greatest revelations that men had ever received. There the disciples saw the transcendent glory that belongs to Jesus Christ which one day will be revealed to the world when He reigns in His kingdom. As the disciples stood in the presence of the Lord while He prayed, the fashion of His countenance was altered and His raiment was white and glistening and Luke records in 9:32, "They saw his glory." In the light of what had been given to them in Mark 3:14, it might have been concluded that, having received this revelation of His glory, they were to go forth to preach and that this was preparation for their preaching ministry. But in the light of what was given in Mark 3:14 there was something more important than preaching — their own personal fellowship with the Lord Jesus Christ. Before the disciples left the Mount of Transfiguration, we read in Luke 9:35, "There came a voice out of the cloud, saying, This is my beloved Son; hear him." The voice did not say, "This is my beloved Son, go preach Him." That would have been fulfilling the second of the two purposes of the choice of these men — "that he might send them forth to preach." But God was calling to their attention that primarily and preeminently they had been called to be with Him. "This is my beloved Son, hear him."

Does your heart desire to be a disciple of Jesus Christ? Then, will you hear again that which our Lord made preeminent? He chose twelve that they might be *with Him.*

The mind must be open to His truth as He communicates it to us through His Word, and respond to that truth in faith. The heart must receive the love of the One who called us to Himself, and love Him in return with a pure heart fervently. The will must acknowledge His will as it is presented to us in the Word, by the Spirit, and respond to that will in perfect obedience. The life of a disciple is a life that centers in Him. "He chose twelve that they might be with him." Is anything hindering your fellowship with the One who calls you to be His disciple?

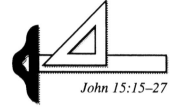

13 The World and the Disciples

John 15:15–27

At the beginning of our Lord's earthly ministry, He appeared to the nation Israel with an arresting message: a message concerning comfort and hope, a message concerning the salvation from sins. Jesus Christ was sent from the Father to reveal the Father to men. He was sent that He might redeem men, and that He might reign over the redeemed. To accomplish that mission which Jesus Christ was sent into the world to perform, He appeared as a preacher. He preached that men might hear and believe.

Our Lord's ministry at the outset attracted great attention and widespread interest. In order that His ministry might be extended throughout the length and the breadth of the land, our Lord chose twelve men. These twelve were chosen that they might fellowship with the Lord and that they, in turn, might be taught by Him to the end that they might go as His witnesses. In the tenth chapter of Matthew, our Lord commissioned the Twelve to go to the lost sheep of the house of Israel. In the seventh verse, He told them, "As ye go, preach." The Twelve were sent out as preachers, proclaimers of the good news that Christ had entrusted to them. Lest they be discouraged and defeated by the response that the nation would give to their message, our Lord warned them as to what they could expect. The disciples were going with the Gospel, that is, good news. The good news was the good news that Christ had come to save sinners. It might reasonably be expected that when such good news was brought to men they would welcome it eagerly and receive the messengers. But such is the hardness of the human heart and so deep is the degradation of the sinner, that when good news is brought to him, he turns against it and also turns against the messenger.

Our Lord, in Matthew 10, reminded these men who were here being sent out that they would be rejected. As sheep in the midst of wolves, they would be defenseless against the onslaughts of the generation to whom they ministered. They would be delivered over to judgment and to jail. Hauled before councils, they would be scourged for the message that they brought. Hated of all men for Christ's sake, they would be killed. They would endure many different forms of persecution. In fact, as one reads through the tenth chapter of Matthew's gospel, one wonders from our Lord's words whether there would be any who would hear and respond favorably to the messengers and their message.

But as the disciples came back after their ministry, they could recount with joy that, even though multitudes rejected, there were those who had responded to the message which they brought. As we pursue our study of the gospels, we see that our Lord, for a season, withdrew these men from a public ministry. They were separated unto the Lord that He might school them in that which He desired to teach them. As we come into that section of the gospels that we call the Upper Room discourse, in John 15, we find our Lord again preparing the disciples to go as His messengers into all the world. The disciples might reasonably have anticipated that, even though Israel as a whole rejected the message which they had brought, when they went to Gentiles the message would be eagerly received and welcomed. A major portion of this discourse is devoted to a preparation of the messengers for the hatred, antagonism, bitterness, rejection, which they would suffer at the hands of those to whom they brought God's good tidings.

The disciple must be prepared to stand alone with the Lord against the world. It is that note of warning that our Lord sounds in John 15: 16. Our Lord says, "Ye have not chosen me, but I have chosen you, and ordained you, that ye should go and bring forth fruit, and that your fruit should remain." These disciples were sovereignly chosen. The Lord had previously selected twelve. Now eleven are left. He is reaffirming a sovereign selection of these men. Not because of the ability, the gifts, the talents which they had, but because it pleased the Father, they were chosen by the Lord. Those who were chosen were ordained by the Lord. An ordination referred to in this verse had to do with setting one apart to a particular work, a special ministry. They had previously been sent out or ordained to preach, and once again they are being set apart, or ordained, that they might declare God's good news to men. Their ordination entails in it a scattering. They are to go, and we would conclude that that which they were to do as they went was the same as that which they were to do as they were sent in Matthew 10:7, where the Lord said, "As ye go, preach." Preaching was an official proclamation by men who had been set apart to that ministry by God, telling the good news that God had entrusted them to deliver. These men did not have to search about for a message, for our Lord had told them in Matthew 10 when they were first sent out that they were to take no thought what they were to say, for what they were to say would be given to them. Our Lord, between Matthew 10 and John 15, has been giving them the message that they are to give to a lost world. It is a message concerning the person and work of Jesus Christ. Now, these men who have been chosen are being set apart to this ministry and are being sent out to become messengers of the good news that has been entrusted to them.

In John 15:26, 27, we find that the men were not being sent out alone, for a divine assistance was promised to those who have been appointed as witnesses. Our Lord had spoken previously in this discourse of the coming of the Comforter, or the coming of the Helper, the divine Assistor sent from God to aid them in the discharge of the work entrusted to them. He reminded them that when the Comforter is come "whom I will send unto you from the Father, even the Spirit of truth, which proceedeth from the Father, he shall testify of me." The Comforter or the Helper is viewed here Himself as a preacher, as a proclaimer of the good news concerning the person and the work of Christ. The Spirit has come that He might reveal Jesus Christ to men and that He might become *the* proclaimer of God's good news to men. Our Lord affirmed this truth later in this discourse in John 16:13 when He said the Spirit "shall not speak of himself; but whatsoever he shall hear, that shall he speak." "He shall glorify me: for he shall receive of mine, and shall shew it unto you." The Spirit of God had come that He might proclaim Jesus Christ to men. Then our Lord adds the words in John 15:27, "Ye also shall bear witness." There are then two witnesses, the believers who are here being commissioned, and the Spirit of God who is sent from the throne of God to work the same work.

Now, the believers assisted by the Holy Spirit might consider themselves invincible and impregnable against the unbelief of the adversaries. But in verses 18 to 25 of John 15, our Lord outlines the antipathy

of the world against these witnesses. He comes to the point bluntly
when He says in verse 18, "If the world hate you [and it most certainly
will], ye know that it hated me before it hated you." The whole world,
John tells us in I John 5, lies comfortably at rest in the lap of the evil
one, self-satisfied, complacent, totally indifferent to its needs before
God, unaware of its lostness, unconvinced of its eternal separation because it is alienated from God, lulled into believing that it will not face
the judgment the Word of God says comes upon an unbeliever. The
worldling does not want to be disturbed. He does not want one to
come and unsettle him in his condition. He does not want one troubling
what he considers to be placid waters. When one comes with a message
concerning Jesus Christ, the worldling responds only one way, that is
by hating both the message and the messenger. This was so to be
anticipated our Lord did not question it. He stated it as an accomplished fact: "if the world hate you [and it most certainly will], ye
know that it hated me before it hated you."

Our Lord, in verses 19 to 24, gives three reasons why the world
will hate the believer. The first is given in verse 19. The world will
hate the believer because the believer has been chosen out of the world.
"If ye were of the world, the world would love his own; but because
ye are not of the world, but I have chosen you out of the world, therefore the world hateth you." Every man born as Adam's son into this
world was born as part of this world's system. He was a citizen of
this world. He was under the headship of the god of this world, that
is Satan. His life centered in the things of Satan. This world was the
sphere in which he lived.

When one receives Jesus Christ as a personal Saviour, he is delivered
from this present world. He is taken out from under the authority,
the headship of the god of this world. He has been delivered from the
curse that rests upon the world, and he has been saved from the judgment that has been meted out by a righteous God upon this world.
"Old things have passed away, behold all things have become new."
And because he has been taken out of all the old associations and has
been separated from the old associates, the old associates hate him
and despise him because of the liberty that he now enjoys in Jesus
Christ. The world can no longer feel at home with him. That which
bound them in fellowship one with another has been separated so that
the ties are broken and they no longer can feel comfortable in the
presence of the one who has been delivered from the curse of this
world.

The only response that is possible on the part of the world is the response of envy and jealousy and consequent hatred because this one has found liberation and they are still in the bonds of iniquity. Our Lord then says the first reason the world will hate them is that they have been chosen out of the world and are no longer in fellowship with it.

The second reason is in verses 20 and 21, "Remember the word that I said unto you, The servant is not greater than his lord. If they have persecuted me, they will also persecute you; if they have kept my saying, they will keep yours also. But all these things will they do unto you for my name's sake." The Lord Jesus had been telling these disciples in this discourse that He presently was to leave them and go into the presence of the Father. If the disciples who believed Him could not go where He is going, it is certainly true that those who did not believe Him could not go where He was going. The unbelievers who rejected Jesus Christ and hated Him without a cause would not give up their hatred of Christ but Christ would not be personally present so they could vent their hatred on Him nor could they go where He was; so they must find a substitute whom they can hate to continue their hatred of Jesus Christ. The world hates Christ; and that hatred is no less diminished today after 2,000 years than it was when Christ walked here among men. The hatred of the world put Jesus Christ to death on the cross. The world hates Him as much now as it hated Him then and hatred cannot be stored up. Hatred must be vented and there must be an object against which that hatred is poured out. Since the world cannot approach Jesus Christ nor touch Jesus Christ, the world hates those who belong to Jesus Christ. You as a believer in Jesus Christ must expect the hatred of the world because the world must vent its stored up hatred of the altogether Lovely One.

The third reason is found in verses 22 - 24, where Christ said, "If I had not come and spoken unto them, they had not had sin; but now they have no cloak [or covering or pretext] for their sin. . . . If I had not done among them the works which none other man did, they had not had sin [that is, had a knowledge of sin]: but now have they both seen and hated both me and my Father." The world hated Christ primarily because He exposed them to themselves. He revealed to them that they were sinners. He revealed to them that they were unlike God, they were unholy and they were unrighteous, and they had no covering for their sins. When Jesus Christ turned the spotlight of divine holiness on their sins, they writhed and rebelled against the One who stripped away the darkness that enveloped them and exposed their ungodliness in the light of the holiness of God. Instead of turning in faith to the One who offered them salvation for sin, they turned in wrath against the One who exposed their sin. The world hated Christ because He revealed the iniquity of the human heart and laid bare their ungodliness. The world still hates the believer who by a godly life reveals the sin of the sinner and convicts him of unrighteousness.

After our Lord had reminded the disciples of the world's hatred of Him and of the world's hatred against them, He touched in chapter 16, verses 1 and 2, on some of the acts of the world against believers. How will this hatred demonstrate itself? "They shall put you out of the synagogues." They will sever your connection with the nation in which you held citizenship so that you lose every political, economic, social, educational and religious privilege that belonged to you as citizens of the commonwealth of Israel. Because the ties between believers and the world have been broken, the world will exclude believers from its fellowship.

Our Lord continues and says, "And whosoever killeth you will think that he doeth God service." Their word will be rejected, they will be defenseless against the world, they will be delivered to trial, persecuted and even killed for the sake of Jesus Christ. The disciples are being sent in order that they might preach. When they preach, they are to preach Christ. Preaching Christ means that the world will be convicted of sin, of unrighteousness, of ungodliness. The judgment of God upon the unbeliever will be made very clear and plain, and men will respond to the preaching of the disciple today the same way they responded to the preaching of our Lord and of our Lord's disciples in their day. The world has not changed. The world is not a friend of God. It is God's enemy. The world has not come under the authority of Jesus Christ; the world as a system is still in rebellion and rejection against Jesus Christ. The world, because it so freely uses the name of Jesus, is not a friend of His. It hates Christ. It hates God. It hates righteousness and godliness and holiness. When the disciple of Jesus Christ fulfills his obligation as a proclaimer of the good news to men who are under divine judgment, he can anticipate only one response apart from the act of God's grace — that is the hatred of the world for his message, for himself as a messenger, for the One whom he preaches.

Discipleship necessitates a willingness to suffer the hatred of the world for Christ's sake. It involves a willingness to be identified with Jesus Christ even though it means that one be persecuted, be delivered to councils, be hated, yea, and even martyred for the sake of Jesus Christ.

When our Lord said in Matthew 28:19, "Go ye into all the world and preach the gospel," He knew full well what that preaching entailed. It was a requirement for discipleship that a man be willing to assume that obligation and accept all that is involved in assuming the commission that was given to him. We feel today that we have outsmarted God, that we have found a way whereby we can be disciples of Christ and at the same time friends of the world. We have found ways of circumventing the world's hatred so that we can be disciples of Christ and friendly with the world at the same time. But we haven't outsmarted God, we have only deceived ourselves.

The one who heard our Lord give this commission and lay down this requirement for disciples said, "Love not the world, neither the things that are in the world. If any man love the world, the love of the Father is not in him" (I John 2:15). James in chapter 4:4 reminds us that it is true today as it was in our Lord's day that friendship with the world is enmity against God. This is because the world is unchanged in its hatred and one cannot be a friend of the world and join in the hatred of the world against God and still be a true disciple of Jesus Christ. The subtle temptation of Satan that is put before us is the temptation to identify with the world, to be at home with them, to be comfortable in their presence and to find means of making the world comfortable when we are with them. When we as disciples of Jesus Christ try to make a worldling comfortable, we are denying the Lord that bought us because Christ did not send us into the world to make the world comfortable. He sent us into the world with a message to reprove and to rebuke and to exhort, that men who are made uncomfortable by our proclamation of Jesus Christ might be brought face to face with Jesus Christ to the salvation of their souls.

We have adopted our means and methods of infiltrating into the world and making the world perfectly comfortable in our presence, yea, we even covet that the world should welcome us into its midst. The worldling can no more be comfortable with a believer in his presence than you can be comfortable with a festering thorn in your finger. If we try to identify with the world, we deny Jesus Christ. Another temptation is the temptation to veil the light that has been given to us. Light convicts, light exposes, light rebukes; and God has made us as lights in the midst of a crooked and perverted generation. Lest the light blind, lest the light reprove and convict, we try to veil the light. The life and the lips of the child of God hide the truth that the disciple of Jesus Christ was sent to proclaim. One cannot be a disciple of Jesus Christ in truth and veil the light that God has placed within him which is first to reprove a darkened world and then to illuminate its path toward the Saviour.

In Galatians 6:14 the Apostle Paul said, "God forbid that I should glory, save in the cross of our Lord Jesus Christ." If Paul had wanted to drop the cross from his preaching, drop the blood from his message, remove the rebuke, delete condemnation for sin from his spoken word, he could have been acceptable any place in the Greek or Roman world. Had Paul removed that which he had been sent to proclaim, he would have been faithless as a disciple of Jesus Christ. That is why he said he was determined to know nothing among them except Jesus Christ and Him crucified. Many of us live from day to day in a business world where we are surrounded by ungodliness on every hand, and we have accommodated ourselves to it so that there is never a rebuke that comes from us for any of the forms of ungodliness or immorality that we see and are associated with on every hand. Where is the conviction of a godly, holy life that makes men miserable when we are in their presence? Where is the spoken word that pierces as a sword into the heart of a sinner? Yet we call ourselves disciples.

One of the clearest evidences of this is found in the book of Hebrews, where second generation Christians were suffering almost unbearably for their faith in Jesus Christ. That which they were called upon to bear seemed too much for them to endure. They hit upon a happy compromise. They thought that, if they went back into the old system and attended the Temple services and took part in some of the Temple rituals and mingled again with the people, the unbelievers who were persecuting them would open up their arms to receive them, and the persecution would be lifted. The scathing denunciation of the apostle falls on these compromisers and he likens it to a repudiation of Jesus Christ, counting the blood wherewith they were sanctified an unholy thing, and despising the very name of the One who had redeemed them.

We have not learned the lesson that had to be brought home so forcibly to these Hebrews, but by compromise, a veiled testimony, by removal of conviction from life and lip, we make ourselves comfortable with the world and try to make the world comfortable with us. One cannot be a disciple and be in such a compromising position at the same time. Hear the word of the Apostle Paul as he says in II Corinthians 6:17, "Wherefore come out from among them, and be ye separate, saith the Lord." Hear it again in Philippians 2:15, 16, "Be blameless and harmless, the sons of God, without rebuke, in the midst of a crooked and perverted nation, among whom ye shine as lights in the world; Holding forth the word of life." That is the ministry of a disciple, to be separated from among them, and to be blameless and harmless in the midst of them; then to hold forth the word of life to them in spite of the antagonism, the bitterness, the hatred, the persecution that one must endure as a disciple of Jesus Christ.

Child of God, redeemed by faith in Jesus Christ, are you willing to be a disciple of Christ, so committed to Him personally, and so committed to the responsibiliy placed upon you as a disciple to preach and proclaim the Word, that you stand with Him in spite of what the world will pour out upon you?

14 Reckoning with Disciples

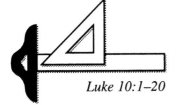

Luke 10:1–20

Those whom our Lord called to be His disciples were indeed a privileged people. Those disciples whom our Lord sent out to be His witnesses were given power to work miracles, to perform signs as Moses and Elijah and Elisha had. To be able to perform miracles put them in a unique and privileged position. When the disciples went out as the Lord's representatives, they were to be supported by those to whom they ministered. This support put them on an equality with the priests of the Old Testament, for the priests were supported by the offerings that were brought by the offerers. This was a privilege. Those who were sent out were to proclaim a message. In this they were equal to the prophets of the Old Testament who declared the Word of God to men. Those who were sent out were to pronounce judgment on unbelievers, and announce acceptance of believers. In this they enjoyed the same privilege that the kings of the Old Testament enjoyed as God's representatives. The chosen few who were called and who responded to Christ's call to become disciples were truly privileged. Every privilege brings a responsibility, and every responsibility brings accountability.

When our Lord in Luke 9 sent the Twelve out as His representatives, they came to report to Him at the conclusion of their ministry. In Luke 9:10 we read: "And the apostles, when they were returned, told him all that they had done." Privileged? Yes. Responsible in view of the privileges? Yes. Accountable for their appointment? Yes.

Thus they returned from their ministry to give a report to the Master who had sent them. In Luke 10 we find that our Lord is expanding the number of witnesses who are to go out through the length and breadth of the land of Israel, and announce to them that God had fulfilled His covenant promise and sent the Messiah to redeem and to reign. God's method of calling workers is a rather unique one, for our Lord did not embark upon a public enlistment campaign. Our Lord said in Luke 10:2: "The harvest truly is great, but the labourers are few." This is an accepted fact for all men need to hear the Word of the Gospel, the Good News that God has sent His Son to redeem sinners. That harvest is great, but it is also true that the laborers who carry the Gospel to men who need to hear the good news are very, very few.

To increase the number of the messengers, our Lord did not resort to a selling campaign, a pressure program, an enlistment drive. Our Lord's method of raising up workers was: "Pray ye therefore the Lord of the harvest, that he would send forth labourers into his harvest." A presentation of human need alone will not enlist workers. God's command to men is that they should go into all the world and preach the Gospel to every creature. But men will not respond to the responsibility placed by the Word of God on those who know Jesus Christ as a personal Saviour. The obligation placed by God on every believer and the appointment of every believer as an ambassador of Jesus Christ does not of itself move men to do that which the Word of God and the Spirit of God command men to do. The only one who can move men to meet the needs of men is the Spirit of God Himself. God has to move men to do that which He commands men to do.

Prayer is an act of dependence on God. In prayer a man acknowledges his helplessness and casts himself upon another who is sufficient. As our Lord looked at the multitudes in unbelief, yet in their great need, He did not try to persuade men to go and bear the good news to them. He enlisted those who knew the program of God and the heart of God, and knew the provision of God, to join with Him in prayer, waiting on God that God would thrust out laborers into the harvest field.

The greatest result that can possibly come from a missionary conference is that the people of God assume an obligation to pray to God on behalf of that work in which God is engaged; and to give themselves to prayer that God would raise up laborers to go into the harvest field to communicate the message. It sounds almost prosaic, but the great need of missions today is not money, although that is great. The greatest need of missions is for laborers, and laborers will not be forthcoming until God moves them. And God's hand will not move until the people of God move the hand of God by prayer. Our Lord solicited the support of those who had been called, and who had responded, to pray the Lord that He would thrust out laborers into His harvest.

Then we find our Lord sent out the seventy, and there is a parallelism between the sending of the Twelve in Luke 9 and the sending of the seventy in Luke 10, for the same message was committed to both, the same means of support given to both, the same authority given to both, the same responsibility placed upon both. Then after the seventy had gone throughout the length and the breadth of the land according to verse 17, they "returned again with joy saying. . . ." They came back to give the Lord a report of the ministry that had been entrusted to them. Having been given the privilege of discipleship, and having assumed the responsibilities of discipleship, they now recognized the accountability of discipleship and, this part of their ministry being ended, they came to give an accounting to the One whose servants they were, the One who had sent them out into the harvest field.

These disciples had received a truth. The truth was that God had sent His Son into the world to save sinners. They had a responsibility to communicate that truth, and, as they went out, they went out to teach and preach and proclaim to all men that message. Now they come to give an accounting of that stewardship that had been placed on them.

It is of the utmost importance that a man realize that when he hears Christ's call to take His yoke upon him and to bear his cross and responds to that call and commits himself to Jesus Christ as a disciple, he is assuming an obligation for which he will be held responsible by God. When a man accepts the privileges of discipleship, he must know that he also accepts the responsibilities of discipleship and must face the accountability of discipleship.

To emphasize this truth, our Lord told a number of parables. We direct you briefly to several of them in order that the Spirit of God might bring to hearts the truth that one day we who have committed ourselves willfully, voluntarily to Jesus Christ to become His disciples, must stand before Him whose call we received and to which call we responded, and give an account of our discipleship.

Turn, first of all, in Luke 19 to the parable recorded in verses 11 -27. In its primary interpretation our Lord is teaching a truth concerning His Old Testament people, Israel, who had been chosen by

God, had received a revelation from God, were commissioned by God to bear the good news of God's truth to the nations of the earth, to which responsibility they were faithless. But in this parable our Lord states a truth that is applicable to us who today have heard His call, "Come unto me, all ye that labour and are heavy laden, and I will give you rest. Take my yoke upon you, and learn of me; for I am meek and lowly in heart: and ye shall find rest unto your souls." As you have heard our Lord's invitation and have responded to it and have said, "I give myself to You to be Your disciple," by that act of commitment you have assumed an obligation for which you are responsible and answerable to God.

Our Lord told of a nobleman who was to leave the scene of his authority for a season. He went into a far country to be absent for awhile before his return. Before his departure, he called ten servants and to these he delivered ten pounds, to each servant a pound, with the instructions, "Occupy [or use this for my benefit] until I come." The nobleman's treasure was committed to these ten men. The fact that there were ten pounds to be distributed among ten men shows us that our Lord is emphasizing the fact that each one had an equal opportunity, each one received the same amount, each one received the same appointment, each one had the same responsibility. After his departure, the ten were busy doing business for the nobleman. At his return, they were called to account concerning the stewardship of that treasure that had been entrusted to them. We read in verse 15: "It came to pass, that when he was returned, having received the kingdom, then he commanded these servants to be called unto him, to whom they had given the money, that he might know how much every man had gained by trading." Each one who had received this responsibility must face the Master who called him and commissioned him.

We see there are varying responses to the responsibility. The first came and said, "Thy pound hath gained ten pounds." This one, because of his faithfulness to his responsibility, was given a reward. He was brought to a position of authority in his master's kingdom and he was to rule over ten cities. The second came and reported that his pound had gained five pounds. He was found faithful and was rewarded for his faithfulness, and had authority under the nobleman to rule over five cities. Finally, he came to the last who was found faithless for he had to report, "Lord, behold, here is thy pound, which I have kept laid up in a napkin." This faithless one was deprived of any reward. His faithlessness excluded him from the king's presence.

This one, who had the same privileges as the ones who had reported previously, was faithless to his privilege. It was not the reception of a treasure that made him a true disciple. It was the faithful use of that which had been deposited with him that made him eligible for a reward. This one heard the master's pronouncement: "Take from him the pound, and give it to him that hath ten pounds. . . . unto every one which hath shall be given; and from him that hath not, even that which he hath shall be taken away from him." This man not only lost his reward, he lost also the privilege of serving the master that had originally been entrusted to him. The misuse of the privileges of discipleship will remove one from the enjoyment of those privileges. Loss of opportunity is the penalty for faithlessness.

In like vein, our Lord taught another parable. This is recorded in Matthew 25:14-30. The situation is similar. Our Lord told of a man traveling into a far country. In preparation for his time away from his country, he called his own servants and delivered to them his goods. One servant received five talents, another servant received two talents, and another servant one talent. Whereas in the parable of the pounds we have the emphasis on equal opportunity to serve, in the parable of the talents through the fact of unequal distribution, we find that the Lord is emphasizing individual privileges and individual responsibilities. In the administration of the affairs of the Master, one man received five talents, another two and another one. Verse 15 tells us that distribution was made according to individual ability. There were some chosen to greater responsibilities, to greater privileges, than others. Each man had an opportunity but there were individual responsibilities. This emphasizes the fact developed by the Apostle Paul, in such passages as Romans 12 or I Corinthians 12, that everyone born 7-11 into the family of God today has a spiritual gift. No member of God's family is without some spiritual gift, but not all have the same gift. There are some gifts that carry a greater burden of responsibility than other gifts. Not all men who are disciples will serve in the same capacity. Every disciple has a responsibility to serve, equal opportunity, but the service which the disciples perform will vary. In the parable of the talents, our Lord is emphasizing the varying responsibilities assigned to those who have committed themselves to Jesus Christ to be His disciples.

As the parable proceeds, we see that each man used that treasure that had been deposited with him in a different way, as in the parable of the pounds. In the nineteenth verse, it is recorded, "After a long time the lord of those servants cometh, and reckoneth with them."

The recipients of the talents had to give an account of their steward-ship.

You are familiar with this well-known story. Two of the men were found faithful; the one who had received five had gained another five; and the one who had received two had gained two. Even though numerically there is a different response, you will see that both have doubled that which the Lord gave to them. With joy, they can report their faithfulness to the Master as good stewards. In each case, our Lord said, "Well done, good and faithful servant; thou hast been faith-ful over a few things, I will make thee ruler over many things: enter thou into the joy of thy Lord." Will you notice a singular thing: our Lord did not give a far greater reward to the five-talent man who had doubled his than He did to the two-talent man who had doubled his. They were equally rewarded because they were equally faithful even though the result of the one was greater. Then came the man who had received the one talent. He had had an opportunity to double his as the two-talent man had doubled his, or the five-talent man had doubled his. The one-talent man did not have as his excuse that he had re-ceived only one talent, he still had the opportunity but he hadn't used it. Our Lord pronounced judgment on him, not because he had not turned back ten talents, but because he had not been faithful. Had he offered two talents, he would have had the same reward as the man who had ten talents to turn over to Christ as the result of his steward-ship. Our Lord said, "Thou wicked and slothful servant . . . thou oughtest therefore to have put my money to the exchangers, and then at my coming I should have received mine own with usury. Take therefore the talent from him, and give it unto him which hath ten talents."

In these two illustrations, our Lord is trying to impress upon those who called themselves His disciples that this call to discipleship and the response to that call entails an obligation. To say to Christ, "I am willing to take up Your cross and follow You," or to say to Christ, "I present my body to You as a living sacrifice," is not the end — it is the beginning. Such a commitment of the will to be a disciple makes one a disciple but we become a disciple to face a future day of reckoning.

Notice what our Lord said in the twelfth chapter of Luke, where once again He refers in verses 47 and 48 to a faithless servant. "That servant, which knew his lord's will, and prepared not himself, neither did according to his will, shall be beaten with many stripes. But he that knew not, and did commit things worthy of stripes, shall be beaten with few stripes. For unto whomsoever much is given, of him shall be much required: and to whom men have committed much, of him they will ask the more." Speaking to a faithless nation which had been called to be a steward of the truth of God, the Lord laid down a principle here that we do well to observe.

God has revealed His truth to us. This truth is recorded in the Word. Perhaps you have heard the Word of God preached and taught for years. To you much has been committed. The knowledge that God has given you of His Word puts a responsibility upon you that cannot be discharged apart from faithfulness to the One who has revealed Himself to you through the Scriptures. God has given you privileges which place responsibilities upon you, and God demands faithfulness on your part commensurate with the gifts that He has given you and the knowledge of Himself He has revealed to you through the Word. The day will come when the Master will call you, His disciples, to an account of your discipleship; and you will fall into one of two classes: faithful or faithless. Christ, who has given the call to men to identify with Him and to become His disciples, said that the mark of disciple-ship is love for the brethren. God will ask you as His disciple whether you have been faithful to this responsibility — or faithless.

He demanded that the disciple count all his material things as belonging to God, and that he is only God's steward of these material things. God will call you to account as to whether you have been faithful to Him in the stewardship of material things He has entrusted to you, or whether you have been faithless.

Christ calls His disciples to separation from the world. One day He will examine your discipleship to see whether you have conformed to and have been a servant of the world, or whether you have been separated to Him.

As a disciple, He has committed the truth of God to you through the Word. He expects the disciple to know the Word, and He will ask you how much of the Word you have learned and what you know and have appropriated. He asks the disciple to obey the Word. The day will come when He will sit in judgment on your obedience to the 1 COR. 3 Word of God to determine whether you are found faithful or faithless.

He calls upon the disciple to be His representative to proclaim the Good News that He came to die for sinful men. One day He will call you before Him and say, "I committed My Gospel to you to tell men what I did for them. What did you do with that commitment?" Are you faithful or faithless?"

The Apostle Paul teaches us the same truth in I Corinthians 3:13 where he tells us, "Every man's work shall be made manifest [revealed]:

for the day shall declare it, because it shall be revealed by fire; and the fire shall try every man's work of what sort it is. If any man's work abide which he has built thereon, he shall receive a reward. If any man's work shall be burned, he shall suffer loss: but he himself shall be saved; yet so as by fire." Again, in II Corinthians 5:9: "We labour, that, whether present or absent, we may be approved [or accepted] of him. For we must all appear before the judgment seat of Christ; that every one may receive the things done in his body, according to that which he hath done, whether it be good or bad." Do you call yourself a disciple of Jesus Christ? Have you committed yourself to Him to do His will? Then may the Word of God impress upon your hearts this fact that God has accepted your commitment, and He has placed a responsibility on you and one day you must give an account of your discipleship.

I trust that the Spirit of God will impress upon you the fact that, having received an appointment as a steward, you must report to Him concerning your faithfulness or faithlessness. Every privilege brings a responsibility, and every responsibility an accountability.

0123456789 abcdef abcdef 1234